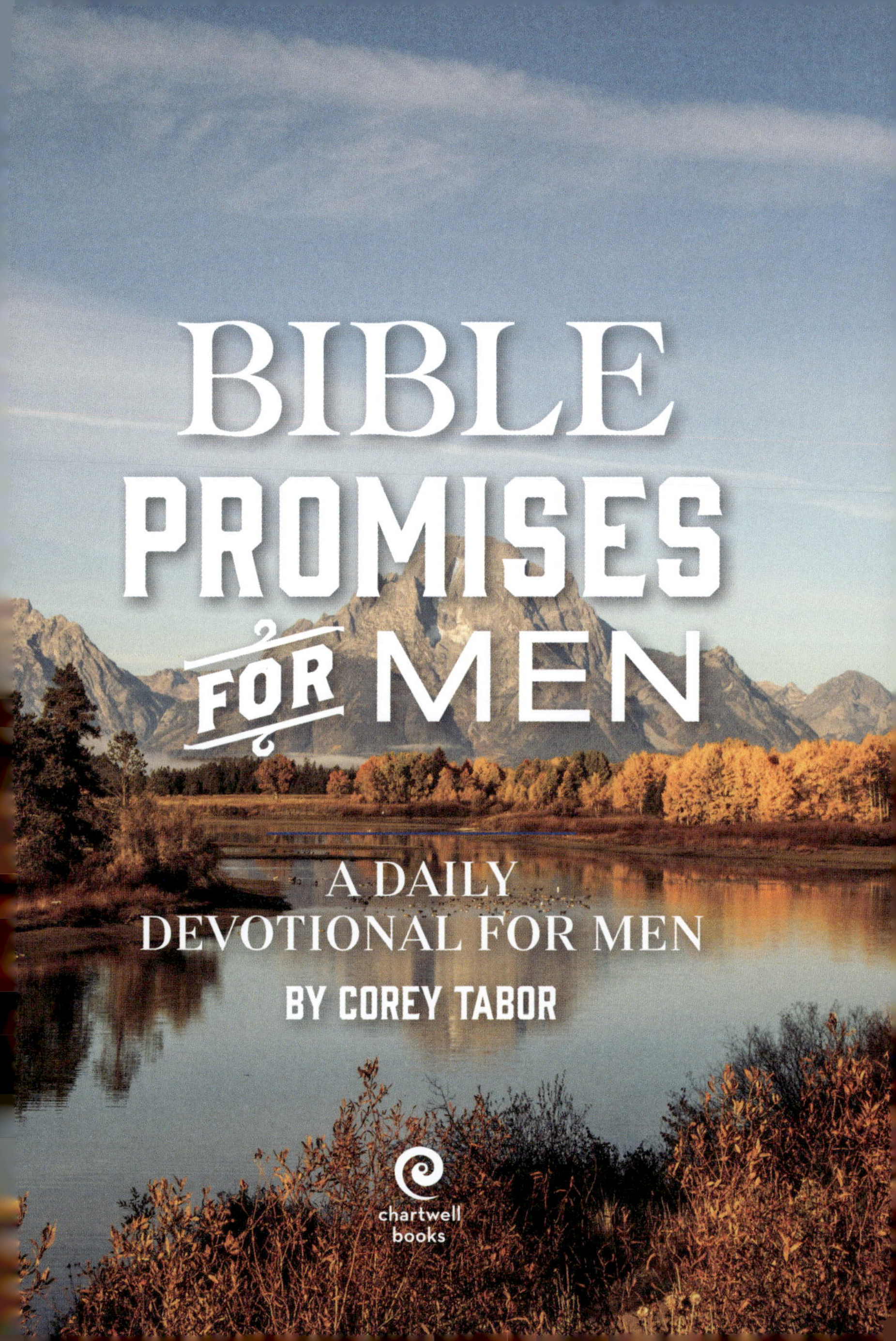

BIBLE PROMISES FOR MEN

A DAILY DEVOTIONAL FOR MEN

BY COREY TABOR

chartwell books

Quarto

This edition published in 2025 by Chartwell Books,
an imprint of The Quarto Group
142 West 36th Street, 4th Floor
New York, NY 10018 USA
T (212) 779-4972
www.Quarto.com

10 9 8 7 6 5 4 3 2 1

Chartwell titles are also available at discount for retail, wholesale, promotional, and bulk purchase. For details, contact the Special Sales Manager by email at specialsales@quarto.com or by mail at The Quarto Group, Attn: Special Sales Manager, 100 Cummings Center Suite 265D, Beverly, MA 01915, USA.

Library of Congress Control Number: 2025944458

ISBN: 978-0-7858-4796-0

Publisher: Wendy Friedman
Publishing Director: Meredith Mennitt
Editor: Joanne O'Sullivan
Designer: Angelika Piwowarczyk
Image credits: Shutterstock

Printed in China

EEA Representation, WTS Tax d.o.o.,
Žanova ulica 3, 4000 Kranj, Slovenia.
www.wts-tax.si

CONTENTS

INTRODUCTION

Growing up, most of us probably got used to promises being made by our parents, teachers, coaches, or even pastors. *If you clean your room, you can go out and play. If you finish your homework, you can have free time. If you practice hard, you'll start next week. If you follow Jesus, he will give you eternal life.* The promises were simple but profound in that we learned promises learned are promises kept. *"For no matter how many promises God has made, they are "Yes" in Christ. And so, through him, the "Amen" is spoken by us to the glory of God"* (2 Corinthians 1:20).

Over time, people began to let us down. A parent promised to pick us up from school and forgot. A teacher promised a field trip that was cancelled due to weather. Our coach found another favorite player for our position. A pastor didn't tell us that sometimes God's answer to prayer is no. Eventually, we started to project the humanity of others onto our heavenly father.

My prayer is that as you read this book, you're reminded that God is a promise keeper and he positions you to experience his goodness in the midst of all that life may throw your way.

There will be times when you question your faith and wonder if God can be trusted. During those seasons, know that he is trustworthy and he can handle your questions. There will be times when you will question your value as a man because of something that happens at your job. But remember, your value is based on who you are and not just what you do. There will be times where you feel as if your loved ones don't respect you and your friends don't understand you; that will be a time to recall the truths of God's promises.

Each topic covered will give you insights into God's word where he communicates his promises which are always true. May you be reminded of the ways God has kept his promises in the past, building your faith for how he will keep his promises in the future.

Prayer

GOD,

THANK YOU FOR BEING MY HEAVENLY FATHER. AS I SEEK TO CONNECT WITH YOU THROUGH YOUR WORD AND PRAYER, I ASK YOU TO OPEN MY EYES TO WALK IN THE TRUTH OF SCRIPTURE. HELP ME BE REMINDED OF YOUR CHARACTER; THAT YOU ARE FAITHFUL, JUST, GRACIOUS, AND LOVING. HELP ME TO TRUST YOU WHEN I CANNOT TRACE YOU, KNOWING YOU ARE PRESENT IN EVERY MOMENT AND SEASON IN MY LIFE.

IN JESUS' NAME, AMEN

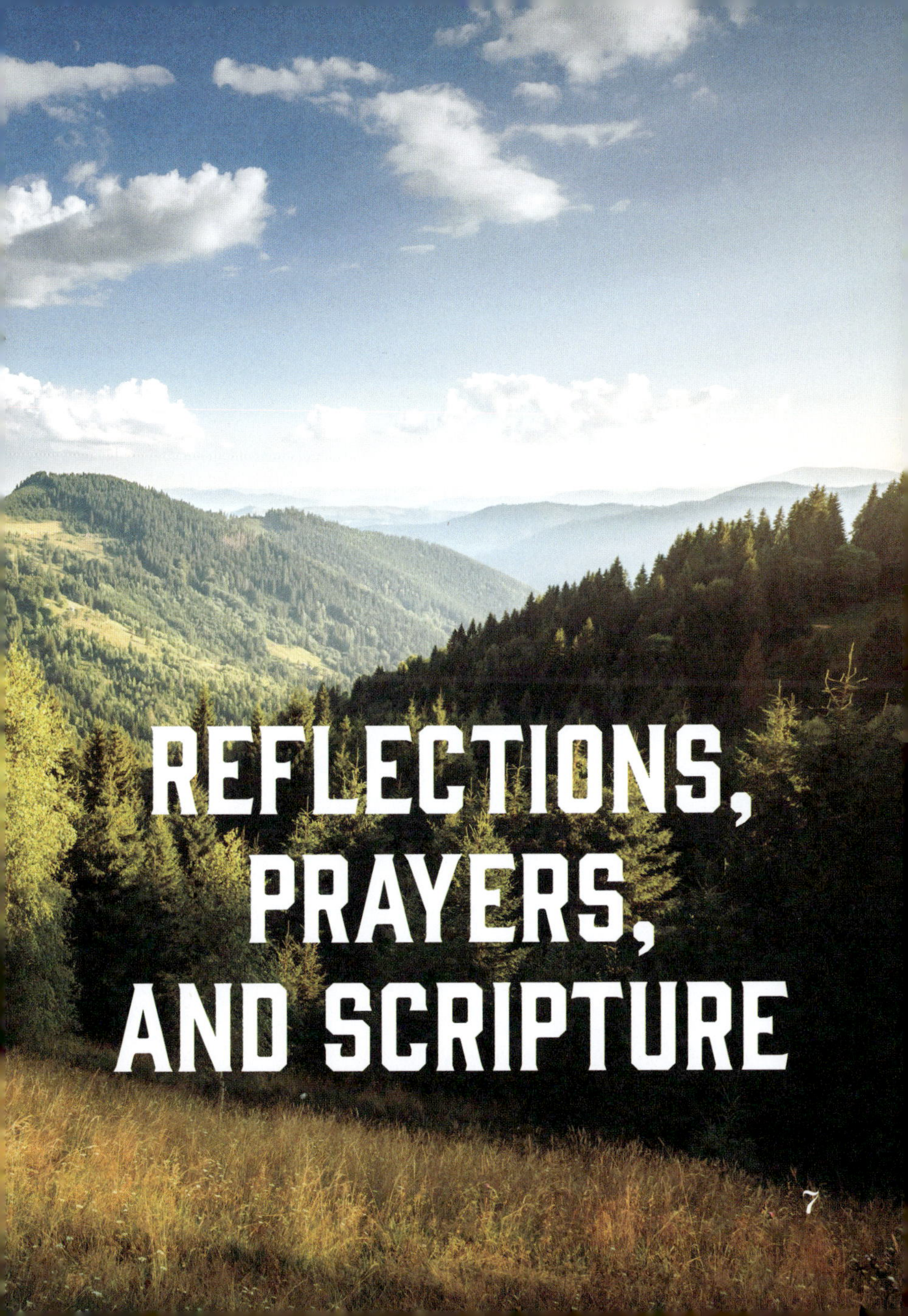

REFLECTIONS, PRAYERS, AND SCRIPTURE

FAITH

Daily, we demonstrate faith in objects that have no power or life. We sit in a chair, having faith it will hold us up. We push the start button in our cars, having faith that they will start. We cook food trusting in its nutritional value. We live by faith naturally every day. As men, we struggle to trust what we cannot see. We study past patterns and allow them to shape our thoughts about the future. We tend to be logical, needing facts to believe some things are possible. God is giving us an opportunity each day to have faith that he is who he says he is and he will do what he says he will do. He gently invites us to have faith in him.

Prayer

FAITHFUL FATHER,

INTELLECTUALLY, I KNOW I HAVE FAITH IN YOU BUT PRACTICALLY, I DON'T ALWAYS LIVE THAT WAY. HELP ME TO HAVE FAITH THE SIZE OF A MUSTARD SEED, SO I CAN SEE MOUNTAINS IN MY LIFE MOVE FOR YOUR GLORY AND MY GOOD.

AMEN

I have fought a good fight, I have finished my course, I have kept the faith.

2 TIMOTHY 4:7

Now faith is the substance of things hoped for, the evidence of things not seen.

HEBREWS 11:1

"Where is your faith?," he asked his disciples. In fear and amazement, they asked one another, "Who is this? He commands even the winds and the water, and they obey him."

LUKE 8:25

He replied, “Because you have so little faith. Truly I tell you, if you have faith as small as a mustard seed, you can say to this mountain, ‘Move from here to there,’ and it will move. Nothing will be impossible for you.”

MATTHEW 17:20

For we live by faith, not by sight.

2 CORINTHIANS 5:7

PATIENCE

Being a parent of young children tests your patience in ways that you're not ready for. Children ask questions and want an immediate answer. Children ask for something from the refrigerator and want it right now. Children can't wait for Christmas to come so they can get what they've asked for. Sometimes we're like little children, struggling to be patient with God, our wives, our kids, our co-workers, or our friends. We struggle to be patient with God as he works in our life to complete the purpose he's begun. Patience is a gift that we can slowly unwrap because it's the gift that keeps on giving as we learn to wait in faith knowing God will keep his promises.

Prayer

LOVING GOD,

THANK YOU FOR THE WAYS YOU'VE BEEN PATIENT WITH ME WHEN I'VE MADE MISTAKES INTENTIONALLY AND UNINTENTIONALLY. HELP ME TO DEVELOP PATIENCE FOR MYSELF AND THOSE AROUND ME SO I CAN BE MORE LIKE YOU.

AMEN

Be patient, then, brothers and sisters, until the Lord's coming. See how the farmer waits for the land to yield its valuable crop, patiently waiting for the autumn and spring rains. You too, be patient and stand firm, because the Lord's coming is near.

JAMES 5:7

My dear brothers and sisters, take note of this: Everyone should be quick to listen, slow to speak and slow to become angry, because human anger does not produce the righteousness that God desires.

JAMES 1:19–20

To those who by persistence in doing good seek glory, honor and immortality, he will give eternal life.

ROMANS 2:7

Love is patient, love is kind. It does not envy, it does not boast, it is not proud.

1 CORINTHIANS 13:4

A hot-tempered person stirs up conflict, but the one who is patient calms a quarrel.

PROVERBS 15:18

SACRIFICE

In the Bible, to sacrifice means giving something of value to God as an act of worship, devotion, or penance. As men, we give a lot of our time and talent to earn treasure as providers in our homes. We may sacrifice sleep to work or sacrifice our desires so our wives or children can have things they need. Our choice to sacrifice is similar to the choice that Jesus made to give his life for our sins. We are not Jesus, but we can model his love by sacrificially giving so others can benefit. As a result, we see our character and influence grow to bless us to be the men we're called to be.

Prayer

GOD,

YOU LOVED THE WORLD SO MUCH THAT YOU GAVE YOUR ONE AND ONLY SON TO DIE ON THE CROSS FOR US. HELP ME TO LAY MY LIFE DOWN SACRIFICIALLY KNOWING THAT WHEN I DO, I AM LIVING IN A WAY THAT HONORS YOU.

AMEN

For it has been granted to you on behalf of Christ not only to believe in him, but also to suffer for him.

PHILIPPIANS 1:29

But even if you should suffer for what is right, you are blessed. Do not fear their threats; do not be frightened.

1 PETER 3:14

I will sacrifice a freewill offering to you; I will praise your name, Lord, for it is good.

PSALMS 54:6

Just as people are destined to die once, and after that to face judgment, so Christ was sacrificed once to take away the sins of many; and he will appear a second time, not to bear sin, but to bring salvation to those who are waiting for him.

HEBREWS 9:27–28

Whoever sacrifices to any god other than the Lord must be destroyed.

EXODUS 22:20

GRATITUDE

Children ask for what they need without thinking about it, but they have to be taught to say 'please' and 'thank you.' Gratitude lets the giver know you appreciate the gift, and it keeps you from becoming entitled, assuming someone has to do something for you. As men we often think of what we still need to get instead of remembering what we already have. I encourage you to write a list of three things for which you're thankful every morning. The attitude of gratitude will improve your mental and emotional state for the entire day, but more than anything, it will remind you of how good God has been to you. As you think about the blessings you've received, you'll find yourself being more content and willing to give from what you've been given.

Prayer

GOD,

THANK YOU FOR THE GIFT OF A RELATIONSHIP WITH YOU THROUGH YOUR SON, JESUS. THANK YOU FOR GIVING ME LIFE AND BREATHE TO LIVE OUT THIS DAY. HELP ME TO PRACTICE GRATITUDE THROUGHOUT THE DAY KNOWING THAT EACH DAY IS A GIFT I'VE BEEN GIVEN. HELP ME TO CHERISH THE GIFT AND MAKE THE MOST OF IT, TODAY.

AMEN

You shall rejoice in all the good things the Lord your God has given to you and your household.

DEUTERONOMY 26:11

All this is for your benefit, so that the grace that is reaching more and more people may cause thanksgiving to overflow to the glory of God.

2 CORINTHIANS 4:15

I have not stopped giving thanks for you, remembering you in my prayers.

EPHESIANS 1:16

Let the message of Christ dwell among you richly as you teach and admonish one another with all wisdom through psalms, hymns, and songs from the Spirit, singing to God with gratitude in your hearts.

COLOSSIANS 3:16

Therefore, since we are receiving a kingdom that cannot be shaken, let us be thankful, and so worship God acceptably with reverence and awe, for our "God is a consuming fire."

HEBREWS 12:28–29

RIGHTEOUSNESS

Have you ever been at odds with a member of your family? You may be related, but you're not close to each other due to some disagreement or offense. Righteousness in scripture speaks to being in right relationship with God. We're righteous not because of what we've done but because of what he did in sending his son Jesus to die for our sins and pay the penalty that was owed. Even when we feel far from God, we are considered righteous because of what Jesus did for us. When we live out of our right standing, we can enjoy the benefits of being a child of God.

Prayer

GOD,

THANK YOU FOR MAKING ME RIGHTEOUS THROUGH THE BLOOD OF JESUS THAT WAS SHED FOR ME. I STAND IN AGREEMENT WITH THE TRUTH OF SCRIPTURE WHICH LETS ME KNOW THAT MY HUMAN RIGHTEOUSNESS IS FILTHY RAGS BUT MY RIGHTEOUSNESS THROUGH CHRIST IS PURE AND COMPLETE. I CHOOSE TO LIVE IN THIS TRUTH TODAY.

AMEN

The righteous cry out, and the Lord hears them; he delivers them from all their troubles.

PSALMS 34:17

Whoever pursues righteousness and love finds life, prosperity and honor.

PROVERBS 21:21

Blessed are those who act justly, who always do what is right.

PSALMS 106:3

All of us have become like one who is unclean, and all our righteous acts are like filthy rags; we all shrivel up like a leaf, and like the wind our sins sweep us away.

ISAIAH 64:6

For I tell you that unless your righteousness surpasses that of the Pharisees and the teachers of the law, you will certainly not enter the kingdom of heaven.

MATHEW 5:20

WORK

As men, we were made to work and to worship, but often our identities are based on our work. When we meet a man, he will often tell us what he does before he tells us who he is or where he is from, because work is core to who we are. There is nothing like completing a good day's work, coming home a little tired but feeling accomplished because we used our gifts and talents to make a difference in the world. I want to challenge us to work, but see it as worship knowing that it honors God.

Prayer

GOD,

HELP ME TO SEE WORK AS AN OPPORTUNITY TO HONOR YOU WITH THE GIFTS YOU'VE GIVEN ME. I KNOW THAT WHEN I WORK, I AM LIKE YOU IN THAT YOU WORKED SIX DAYS CREATING THE WORLD BUT ON THE SEVENTH DAY YOU RESTED. I PRAY THAT I FIND THE BALANCE NEEDED TO WORK AND REST IN RHYTHM WITH YOU.

AMEN

The sleep of a laborer is sweet, whether they eat little or much, but as for the rich, their abundance permits them no sleep.

ECCLESIASTES 5:12

The LORD God took the man and put him in the Garden of Eden to work it and take care of it.

GENESIS 2:15

The one who plants and the one who waters have one purpose, and they will each be rewarded according to their own labor.

1 CORINTHIANS 3:8

"My food," said Jesus, "is to do the will of him who sent me and to finish his work."

JOHN 4:34

Now we ask you, brothers and sisters, to acknowledge those who work hard among you, who care for you in the Lord and who admonish you. Hold them in the highest regard in love because of their work. Live in peace with each other.

1 THESSALONIANS 5:12–13

COMPASSION

The hard shell that we often display as men to protect us from getting hurt can get in the way of being tenderhearted and compassionate. It's easy to judge a person who is in a challenging situation financially, assuming they didn't work hard enough or manage their money well. It's easy to be critical of someone going through a divorce or losing their job. But the heart of our father is compassionate. To be like him, we must tap into empathy that allows us to not only put ourselves in someone else's shoes but do what we would hope someone would do for us, be compassionate.

Prayer

HEAVENLY FATHER,

I AM GRATEFUL FOR THE COMPASSION YOU HAVE SHOWN ME IN TIMES IN MY LIFE WHERE I DESERVED JUDGEMENT AND YOU GAVE ME MERCY. GROW MY HEART TO BE COMPASSIONATE AS JESUS WAS WHEN HE SAW THE PEOPLE WITHOUT A SHEPHERD AND CHOSE TO CARE DEEPLY AND WAS MOVED TO ACTION. I ASK FOR YOU TO BREAK MY HEART FOR THE THINGS THAT BREAK YOUR HEART.

IN JESUS' NAME, AMEN

May the Lord make your love increase and overflow for each other and for everyone else, just as ours does for you.

1 THESSALONIANS 3:12

Do not gloat when your enemy falls; when they stumble, do not let your heart rejoice.

PROVERBS 24:17

Defend the weak and the fatherless; uphold the cause of the poor and the oppressed.

PSALMS 82:3

And the Lord said, “I will cause all my goodness to pass in front of you, and I will proclaim my name, the Lord, in your presence. I will have mercy on whom I will have mercy, and I will have compassion on whom I will have compassion.”

EXODUS 33:19

When Jesus landed and saw a large crowd, he had compassion on them, because they were like sheep without a shepherd. So, he began teaching them many things.

MARK 6:34

DOUBT

Have you ever tried to lose weight by exercising but not managing your diet? It doesn't work. You cannot outwork your diet because nutrition is the foundation to physical health. The same is true when it comes to faith. It's hard to build the spiritual muscle of faith while eating large doses of doubt every day. We can't please God without faith because he wants us to trust him fully. I encourage you to check every doubtful thought at the door of your mind, arresting it and replacing it with faith, because that is the God-kind of life Jesus gives. When we doubt, we're living like children.

Prayer

FATHER GOD,

THANK YOU FOR BEING A GOOD FATHER WHO I CAN TRUST. HELP ME NOT DOUBT YOU OR WHAT YOU CAN DO IN MY LIFE. I KNOW THAT DREAM KILLERS SOW SEEDS OF DOUBT, BUT TODAY I WILL PULL THOSE WEEDS BEFORE THEY TAKE ROOT IN MY HEART I CHOOSE TO TRUST YOU.

AMEN

Then Jesus told him, “Because you have seen me, you have believed; blessed are those who have not seen and yet have believed.”

JOHN 20:29

Immediately Jesus reached out his hand and caught him. “You of little faith,” he said, “why did you doubt?”

MATTHEW 14:31

But when you ask, you must believe and not doubt, because the one who doubts is like a wave of the sea, blown and tossed by the wind.

JAMES 1:6

Jesus replied, "Truly I tell you, if you have faith and do not doubt, not only can you do what was done to the fig tree, but also you can say to this mountain, 'Go, throw yourself into the sea,' and it will be done."

MATTHEW 21:21

When they saw him, they worshiped him; but some doubted.

MATTHEW 28:17

HONESTY

In the 1992 film, *A Few Good Men*, Jack Nicholson plays Colonel Nathan R. Jessep. On the witness stand while being interrogated by Tom Cruise playing JAG Corp. Lieutenant Daniel Kaffee, Nicholson shares the famous line, "You can't handle the truth." This statement is a question we need to ask ourselves daily as men. Can I be honest with myself about where I am in life and why I am here? Can I be completely honest with my wife or my boss? Do I trust that they can handle the truth? Theologically and theoretically, we know that truth is always right but it's not always easy. Make a plan to tell the truth today, it will be worth it.

Prayer

JESUS,

YOU SAID YOU WERE THE WAY, THE TRUTH, AND THE LIFE. I PRAY FOR HONEST LIPS AND AN HONEST LIFE THAT IS LIVED WITH INTEGRITY, KNOWING THAT HONESTY HONORS YOU. KEEP ME FROM THE TEMPTATION TO BE DECEPTIVE BASED ON FEARS OF HOW PEOPLE WILL RESPOND TO ME. I PRAY THAT I WILL CARE MORE ABOUT YOUR OPINION THAN THE OPINION OF OTHERS.

AMEN

The righteous hate what is false, but the wicked make themselves a stench and bring shame on themselves.

PROVERBS 13:5

The LORD detests lying lips, but he delights in people who are trustworthy.

PROVERBS 12:22

I have no greater joy than to hear that my children walk in truth.

3 JOHN 1:4

And my honesty will testify for me in the future, whenever you check on the wages you have paid me. Any goat in my possession that is not speckled or spotted, or any lamb that is not dark-colored, will be considered stolen.

GENESIS 30:33

So, justice is driven back, and righteousness stands at a distance; truth has stumbled in the streets, honesty cannot enter.

ISAIAH 59:14

BLESSINGS

In Scripture, the word 'blessings' is usually used to describe favor or fortune. We are blessed with so many things, many of them the immaterial things that make life meaningful. The question we have to ask ourselves as men is "How am I stewarding the blessings I've received?" Are we being generous or living with a scarcity mindset? Are we developing the people around us or stepping over them for the next promotion or opportunity? We've been blessed to be a blessing, so I encourage you to bless someone else with a blessing you've been given.

Prayer

GIVER OF GOOD GIFTS,

YOU HAVE BLESSED ME WITH SO MANY BLESSINGS THAT I HONESTLY CAN'T COUNT THEM ALL. IF I STARTED A LIST, THE PAGE WOULD NOT BE ENOUGH BECAUSE THERE ARE SO MANY. SHOW ME SOMEONE WHO NEEDS TO BE BLESSED BY ME TODAY WITH A KIND WORD, A SIMPLE ACT OF KINDNESS, OR A MATERIAL RESOURCE YOU'VE PLACED IN MY HANDS. I BLESS YOU, JESUS, FOR BLESSING ME.

AMEN

Blessed are all who fear the LORD, who walk in obedience to him.

PSALMS 128:1

Each of you must bring a gift in proportion to the way the LORD your God has blessed you.

DEUTERONOMY 16:17

And God is able to bless you abundantly, so that in all things at all times, having all that you need, you will abound in every good work.

2 CORINTHIANS 9:8

God blessed them and said to them, "Be fruitful and increase in number; fill the earth and subdue it. Rule over the fish in the sea and the birds in the sky and over every living creature that moves on the ground."

GENESIS 1:28

Blessed are the pure in heart, for they shall see God.

MATTHEW 5:8

PRAYER

Prayer is a privilege that we as men should take advantage of consistently. As the scriptures say, we should pray without ceasing. Prayer is a conversation with God during which we can consistently hear him speak to us and we know what he hears us. If we truly believed prayer works, we would pray more. Our prayers are missiles of mercy that can be spread over our friends, family, and co-workers. Our prayers can change the perspective we have on our present and the reality of our future. So, with the promise that God answers prayer, we must actively choose to pray.

Prayer

HEAVENLY FATHER,

THANK YOU FOR HEARING ME WHEN I PRAY. HELP ME TO BRING ALL MY CONCERNS, JOYS, AND PAINS TO YOU IN PRAYER KNOWING THAT NOTHING I SHARE WILL SURPRISE YOU. I COMMIT TO INVITING YOU INTO MY DAYS AND GIVE YOU PERMISSION TO SPEAK INTO MY LIFE SO I CAN BE LED BY YOUR SPIRIT ALL THE DAYS OF MY LIFE.

AMEN

Pray without ceasing.

1 THESSALONIANS 5:17

As for me, I call to God, and the LORD saves me. Evening, morning and noon I cry out in distress, and he hears my voice.

PSALMS 55:16–17

Devote yourselves to prayer, being watchful and thankful. And pray for us, too, that God may open a door for our message, so that we may proclaim the mystery of Christ, for which I am in chains.

COLOSSIANS 4:2-3

Then Jesus told his disciples a parable to show them that they should always pray and not give up.

LUKE 18:1

Then you will call upon me and come and pray to me, and I will hear you.

JEREMIAH 29:12

FRIENDSHIP

I have often heard it said, if you show me your friends, I'll show you your future. Your friends affect what you believe about God, yourself, your spouse, your kids, and the world. The people you spend time with will open your mind or close your mind. I challenge you to do an audit of your friend network and ask are these friends an asset or a liability to your relationship with God? Are they moving closer to God or further away from him? Friends are like an investment. They will produce a dividend; the question is "What will the dividend be?"

Prayer

JESUS,

YOU HAD TWELVE FRIENDS THAT DID LIFE WITH YOU. PETER, JAMES, AND JOHN WERE YOUR CLOSEST FRIENDS; FROM THE MOUNTAIN OF TRANSFIGURATION TO THE GARDEN OF GETHSEMANE, THEY SAW YOUR HIGHS AND YOUR LOWS. I PRAY FOR FRIENDS THAT WILL HELP ME BELIEVE YOU MORE AND TRUST THAT YOU WILL WORK IN AND THROUGH MY LIFE FOR YOUR GLORY.

IN YOUR NAME, AMEN

Two are better than one, because they have a good return for their labor: If either of them falls down, one can help the other up. But pity anyone who falls and has no one to help them up.

ECCLESIASTES 4:9–10

A friend loves at all times, and a brother is born for a time of adversity.

PROVERBS 17:17

Greater love has no one than this: to lay down one's life for one's friends.

JOHN 15:13

My intercessor is my friend as my eyes pour out tears to God.

JOB 16:20

The righteous choose their friends carefully, but the way of the wicked leads them astray.

PROVERBS 12:26

FATHERHOOD

Fatherhood is one of the greatest gifts I've received as a man. There is nothing like seeing your child born in your image and loving them when they have done nothing for you but exist. They can't talk. They can't make money. They can't even see you at first, but they know your voice and they love you already. Being a father has taught me about the heart of our heavenly father, who loves us unconditionally and will move heaven and earth to be in relationship with us; which is why he sent his only son Jesus to die for us. May fatherhood connect you more deeply to the heavenly father.

Prayer

GOD,

THANK YOU FOR BEING MY HEAVENLY FATHER. I KNOW THAT I DON'T ALWAYS GET THIS FATHERHOOD ROLE RIGHT. THERE ARE TIMES WHEN I AM IMPATIENT, ANGRY, FRUSTRATED, OR SIMPLY DISAPPOINTED WITH MYSELF AND MY CHILDREN. HELP ME TO SEE MY CHILDREN THE WAY YOU SEE ME AND HELP ME TO BE A DEMONSTRATION OF YOUR FATHERLY LOVE TO THEM. MAY THEY GROW CLOSER TO YOU BECAUSE I'M GROWING CLOSER TO YOU.

IN JESUS' NAME, AMEN

Fathers, do not embitter your children, or they will become discouraged.

COLOSSIANS 3:21

Children's children are a crown to the aged, and parents are the pride of their children.

PROVERBS 17:6

These commandments that I give you today are to be on your hearts. Impress them on your children. Talk about them when you sit at home and when you walk along the road, when you lie down and when you get up.

DEUTERONOMY 6:6–7

Children are a heritage from the LORD, offspring a reward from him. Like arrows in the hands of a warrior are children born in one's youth. Blessed is the man whose quiver is full of them. They will not be put to shame when they contend with their opponents in court.

PSALMS 127:3–5

So, he got up and went to his father. But while he was still a long way off, his father saw him and was filled with compassion for him; he ran to his son, threw his arms around him and kissed him.

LUKE 15:20

KINDNESS

Kindness is a secret weapon that many men struggle to use. Influence is often desired by men, yet it is gained through kindness. God is love and love is kind. Imagine how today will be different if you intentionally choose to be kind to people in traffic, at the grocery store, or on the golf course. Imagine how pleasant the evening will be if you choose to be kind to your roommate after a long day. Kindness changes the attitude inside and atmosphere outside.

Prayer

JESUS,

YOU DEMONSTRATED KINDNESS IN HEALING THE SICK, RAISING THE DEAD, AND FEEDING THE HUNGRY. YOU CAME TO KINDLY SET PEOPLE FREE FROM BONDAGE TO SIN AND SHAME. I AM ASKING THAT YOU GIVE ME THE ABILITY TO DEMONSTRATE KINDNESS TO THOSE IN MY CIRCLE OF INFLUENCE SO I CAN BE MORE LIKE YOU.

IN YOUR NAME, AMEN

But love your enemies, do good to them, and lend to them without expecting to get anything back. Then your reward will be great, and you will be children of the Most High, because he is kind to the ungrateful and wicked.

LUKE 6:35

The LORD appeared to us in the past, saying: “I have loved you with an everlasting love; I have drawn you with unfailing kindness.”

JEREMIAH 31:3

I am unworthy of all the kindness and faithfulness you have shown your servant. I had only my staff when I crossed this Jordan, but now I have become two camps.

GENESIS 32:10

Therefore be imitators of God, as beloved children. And walk in love, as Christ loved us and gave himself up for us, a fragrant offering and sacrifice to God.

EPHESIANS 5:12

You have heard that it was said, 'Love your neighbor and hate your enemy.' But I tell you, love your enemies and pray for those who persecute you,

MATTHEW 5:43–44

MATERIAL THINGS

As men, we think about material things from an early age. From baseball cards to hot wheel cars; from video game systems to houses and cars, we are wired to conquer and possess. God doesn't mind us having possessions as long as the possessions don't have us. When placed in the right hands and with the right perspective, material things, can be a blessing to us and others but when placed in the wrong hands and with the wrong perspective, they can be fatal. Don't let material things keep you from the main thing: loving God and loving people.

Prayer

GOD,

THANK YOU FOR ALL YOU HAVE BLESSED ME TO POSSESS. I WANT TO REMEMBER THAT I AM A STEWARD OF WHAT I HAVE, NOT AN OWNER. I PRAY THAT I WILL MANAGE WHAT YOU'VE GIVEN ME WITH THE HUMILITY IN WHICH YOU PROVIDED IT FOR ME. HELP ME TO BE CONTENT WITH WHAT YOU'VE PROVIDED AND CONFIDENT THAT YOU WILL CONTINUE TO PROVIDE.

IN YOUR NAME, AMEN

For we brought nothing into this world, and it is certain we can carry nothing out.

1 TIMOTHY 6:7

Peter answered: “May your money perish with you, because you thought you could buy the gift of God with money!”

ACTS 8:20

No one can serve two masters. Either you will hate the one and love the other, or you will be devoted to the one and despise the other. You cannot serve both God and money.

MATTHEW 6:24

Give, and it will be given to you. A good measure, pressed down, shaken together and running over, will be poured into your lap. For with the measure you use, it will be measured to you.

LUKE 6:38

What good is it for someone to gain the whole world, yet forfeit their soul?

MARK 8:36

TEMPTATION

Every man must battle temptation just as Jesus did in the garden, and that same power that he used to defeat temptation lives inside of you. Being a godly man is not about perfection, but the daily pursuit towards sanctification. Just like a battery needing to charge, the longer you plug into God, the stronger your connection to him will be. This strength is needed to overcome temptation because we don't get to determine how intense the temptation will be. However, we do control our response to temptation by learning to flee it.

Prayer

LORD,

CLEANSE MY HEART AND CHANGE ME FROM THE INSIDE OUT. THOUGH I AM TEMPTED, I WILL OVERCOME LIKE JESUS. SHOW ME THE WAY TO ESCAPE WHEN TEMPTED AS I MAKE MY BODY A LIVING SACRIFICE. I PUT TO DEATH ALL DESIRES THAT ARE NOT OF YOU.

IN JESUS' NAME, AMEN

Flee also youthful lusts: but follow righteousness, faith, charity, peace, with them that call on the Lord out of a pure heart.

2 TIMOTHY 2:22

Be alert and of sober mind. Your enemy the devil prowls around like a roaring lion looking for someone to devour.

1 PETER 5:8

Flee from sexual immorality. All other sins a person commits are outside the body, but whoever sins sexually, sins against their own body.

1 CORINTHIAN 6:18

No temptation has overtaken you except what is common to mankind. And God is faithful; he will not let you be tempted beyond what you can bear. But when you are tempted, he will also provide a way out so that you can endure it.

1 CORINTHIANS 10:13

When tempted, no one should say, "God is tempting me." For God cannot be tempted by evil, nor does he tempt anyone.

JAMES 1:13

HUMILITY

Jesus modeled humility for us in ways that we as men can learn from on a daily basis. He was all powerful, yet he chose to use his power for good and not evil. He could have been the most prideful person on the planet, but he practiced humility because he knew where his power came from: his heavenly father. You don't have to be weak to be humble, you just need to understand where your help comes from. Humility honors God and inspires people. Walk humbly with God.

Prayer

GOD,

I KNOW YOU CAN HUMBLE ME, BUT I WANT TO HUMBLE MYSELF BECAUSE I KNOW THAT WHEN I DO, YOU WILL NOT ONLY EXALT ME BUT DO IT IN A WAY THAT WILL BE A BLESSING AND NOT A CURSE. I TRUST THAT YOU KNOW WHAT IS BEST FOR MY LIFE AND HAVE GIVEN ME WHAT I NEED TO BE WHO YOU CALLED ME TO BE. SO, I HUMBLY SUBMIT TO YOUR WILL FOR LIFE TODAY.

AMEN

Humble yourselves, therefore, under God's mighty hand, that he may lift you up in due time.

1 PETER 5:6

Woe unto them that are wise in their own eyes, and prudent in their own sight.

ISAIAH 5:21

Seek the Lord, all you humble of the land, you who do what he commands. Seek righteousness, seek humility perhaps you will be sheltered on the day of the Lord's anger.

ZEPHANIAH 2:3

He has shown you, O mortal, what is good. And what does the Lord require of you? To act justly and to love mercy and to walk humbly with your God.

MICAH 6:8

Such regulations indeed have an appearance of wisdom, with their self-imposed worship, their false humility and their harsh treatment of the body, but they lack any value in restraining sensual indulgence.

COLOSSIANS 2:23

GOD'S ETERNAL LOVE

Love is a word that is often misinterpreted in our society. As men, we say we love our sports teams, which is a different kind of love that we have for our wives or kids. God's love is not temporal or conditional. He doesn't love you because of what you've done, he loves you because you are his child. When you are secure in his love for you, it will give you the confidence to live out of the overflow of his love where people see the heart of the father in you. I challenge you to love as if you received unconditional love, because you have.

Prayer

GOD,

THANK YOU FOR LOVING ME ENOUGH TO SEND YOUR ONLY SON, JESUS. I KNOW THAT I DON'T DESERVE YOUR LOVE, BUT I RECEIVE IT AS THE GIFT THAT YOU MEANT FOR IT TO BE; UNCONDITIONAL. HELP ME TO LOVE OTHERS THE WAY YOU LOVE ME, WITH NO STRINGS ATTACHED. I CHOOSE TO GIVE LOVE AWAY AS YOU GAVE YOUR MATCHLESS LOVE TO ME.

AMEN

Heaven and earth will pass away, but my words will never pass away. But about that day or hour no one knows, not even the angels in heaven, nor the Son, but only the Father.

MATTHEW 24:35–36

The grass withers and the flowers fall, but the word of our God endures forever.

ISAIAH 40:8

But the plans of the Lord stand firm forever, the purposes of his heart through all generations.

PSALMS 33:11

For God so loved the world that he gave his one and only Son, that whoever believes in him shall not perish but have eternal life.

JOHN 3:16

But God demonstrates his own love for us in this: While we were still sinners, Christ died for us.

ROMANS 5:8

BURDENS

As teenagers, we notice hormonal changes in our bodies that allowed us to build muscle and gain weight. We choose to lift burdens known as weights to get stronger and to look better. At 15 years old, we're not as worried about being healthy as we are focused on being attractive to girls and strong enough to dominate the field. Without realizing it, we grow up to be men who carry burdens that aren't ours to carry because God has given us his spirit to carry the load. May your load be lightened today as you allow Jesus to carry it with you.

Prayer

GOD,

FORGIVE ME FOR CARRYING BURDENS THAT AREN'T MINE TO CARRY. I AM CALLED TO WORK, BUT YOU ARE MY PROVIDER. I AM CALLED TO PLAN BUT YOU ARE MY GUIDE. I WANT TO LET YOU CARRY THIS LOAD THAT IS TOO HEAVY FOR ME TO BEAR. MY SHOULDERS AREN'T BROAD ENOUGH, AND MY BACK ISN'T STRONG ENOUGH, SO TAKE THIS BURDEN FROM ME SO I CAN BE FREE.

IN JESUS' NAME, AMEN

Carry each other's burdens, and in this way you will fulfill the law of Christ.

GALATIANS 6:2

For each one should carry their own load.

GALATIANS 6:5

Come to me, all you who are weary and burdened, and I will give you rest.

MATTHEW 11:28

I cannot carry all these people by myself;
the burden is too heavy for me.

NUMBERS 11:14

My guilt has overwhelmed me like a
burden too heavy to bear.

PSALMS 38:4

GENEROSITY

Being generous is a foundational principle in our faith. God gave his only son, which is why he judges generosity from the heart. If you only give when you have an abundance, where is the sacrifice? Being generous not only shows your willingness, but level of trust in God. God promotes generous men. You can be generous beyond finances to your time, talent, or kindness This is good news for godly men, whether you are single or have a family, generosity impacts future generations and has heavenly implications.

Prayer

LORD,

THANK YOU FOR WHAT YOU HAVE PUT IN MY HANDS. WHETHER I HAVE AN ABUNDANCE OR A LITTLE, GIVE ME A GENEROUS HEART. HELP ME TO PRACTICE GENEROSITY WHEN MY HUMANITY FIGHTS AGAINST GIVING. SHOW ME HOW TO BE GENEROUS IN MY EVERYDAY AFFAIRS TO MAKE A LASTING IMPACT. LET THOSE WHO RECEIVE FEEL THE LOVE OF JESUS WITH EVERY GENEROUS ACT. LORD MULTIPLY EVERY GENEROUS SEED FOR YOUR GLORY AND NOT MY OWN.

AMEN

When you make a loan of any kind to your neighbor, do not go into their house to get what is offered to you as a pledge.

DEUTERONOMY 24:10

Each of you should give what you have decided in your heart to give, not reluctantly or under compulsion, for God loves a cheerful giver.

2 CORINTHIANS 9:7

The wicked borrow and do not repay, but the righteous give generously.

PSALMS 37:21

In everything I did, I showed you that by this kind of hard work we must help the weak, remembering the words the Lord Jesus himself said: "It is more blessed to give than to receive."

ACTS 20:35

Give, and it will be given to you. Good measure, pressed down, shaken together, running over, will be put into your lap. For with the measure you use it will be measured back to you.

LUKE 6:38

CHEERFULNESS

The cheer of the Christmas season is contagious. Walking through stores, you hear songs of joy and people are smiling as they hum along. Similarly, when we as men bring cheerfulness to the environments we occupy, we can create a contagious experience of joy. In the same way that cheerleaders encourage the audience to cheer for athletes to go beyond their limitations, we can bring cheerfulness to our co-workers in a way that they look forward to working with us. We can bring cheer to our families in a way that they look forward to us coming home. Tap into the cheerleader that your heavenly father is for you and bring the cheer today.

Prayer

GOD,

WHAT A GIFT IT IS TO CHEERFULLY SERVE YOU AND OTHERS WITH MY DAYS. I ASK FOR CHEER TO BE IN MY HEART AND FLOW TO OTHERS. I ALSO ASK THAT OTHERS' CHEER WOULD BRIGHTEN MY DAY WHEN I AM STRUGGLING TO FIND THE CHEER WITHIN MYSELF.

AMEN

I have told you these things, so that in me you may have peace. In this world you will have trouble. But take heart! I have overcome the world.

JOHN 16:33

But Jesus immediately said to them: “Take courage! It is I. Don’t be afraid.”

MATTHEW 14:27

A cheerful heart is good medicine, but a crushed spirit dries up the bones.

PROVERBS 17:22

If it is to encourage, then give encouragement; if it is giving, then give generously; if it is to lead, do it diligently; if it is to show mercy, do it cheerfully.

ROMANS 12:8

All the days of the oppressed are wretched, but the cheerful heart has a continual feast.

PROVERBS 15:15

LEARNING

Learning is one of the first skills we develop as infants. We learn to nurse. We learn to chew. We learn to crawl. We learn to walk. We learn to smile and to wave. Learning is natural when we are growing. What are you learning right now about God? What are you learning about yourself? What are you learning about the world? Our willingness to learn will keep us able to adjust with the changing times so we remain prepared to impact the world for God. Keep learning as you are led by his Spirit.

Prayer

JESUS,

YOU ARE 'THE GREAT TEACHER' AND I WANT TO BE A GREAT STUDENT. MAY YOUR SPIRIT GUIDE ME INTO ALL TRUTH, ALLOWING ME TO DISCERN BETWEEN WHAT IS GOOD AND WHAT IS BEST FOR MY LIFE. HELP ME TO LEARN YOUR WAYS AND LIVE THEM OUT SO OTHERS CAN SEE YOU THROUGH ME.

IN YOUR NAME, AMEN

But as for you, continue in what you have learned and have become convinced of, because you know those from whom you learned it, and how from infancy you have known the Holy Scriptures, which are able to make you wise for salvation through faith in Christ Jesus.

2 TIMOTHY 3:14–15

Instruct the wise and they will be wiser still; teach the righteous and they will add to their learning.

PROVERBS 9:9

A cheerful heart is good medicine, but a crushed spirit dries up the bones.

PROVERBS 17:22

Brothers and sisters, stop thinking like children. In regard to evil be infants, but in your thinking be adults.

1 CORINTHIANS 14:20

Moses summoned all Israel and said: Hear, Israel, the decrees and laws I declare in your hearing today. Learn them and be sure to follow them.

DEUTERONOMY 5:1

Hear my words, you wise men; listen to me, you men of learning.

JOB 34:2

JUDGEMENT

Law and Order is one of the longest running television shows in history. I think we as men like shows like this because we want to see justice served and judgement rendered. We hate to see people get away with murder, robbery, or fraud. If we're honest, at times we want mercy for ourselves when we want judgement for others. God is our ultimate judge, and we will have to answer to him for how we live our life. May we do so in a way that allows him to judge first on what Christ has done for us and then how we have chosen to steward the life we've been given.

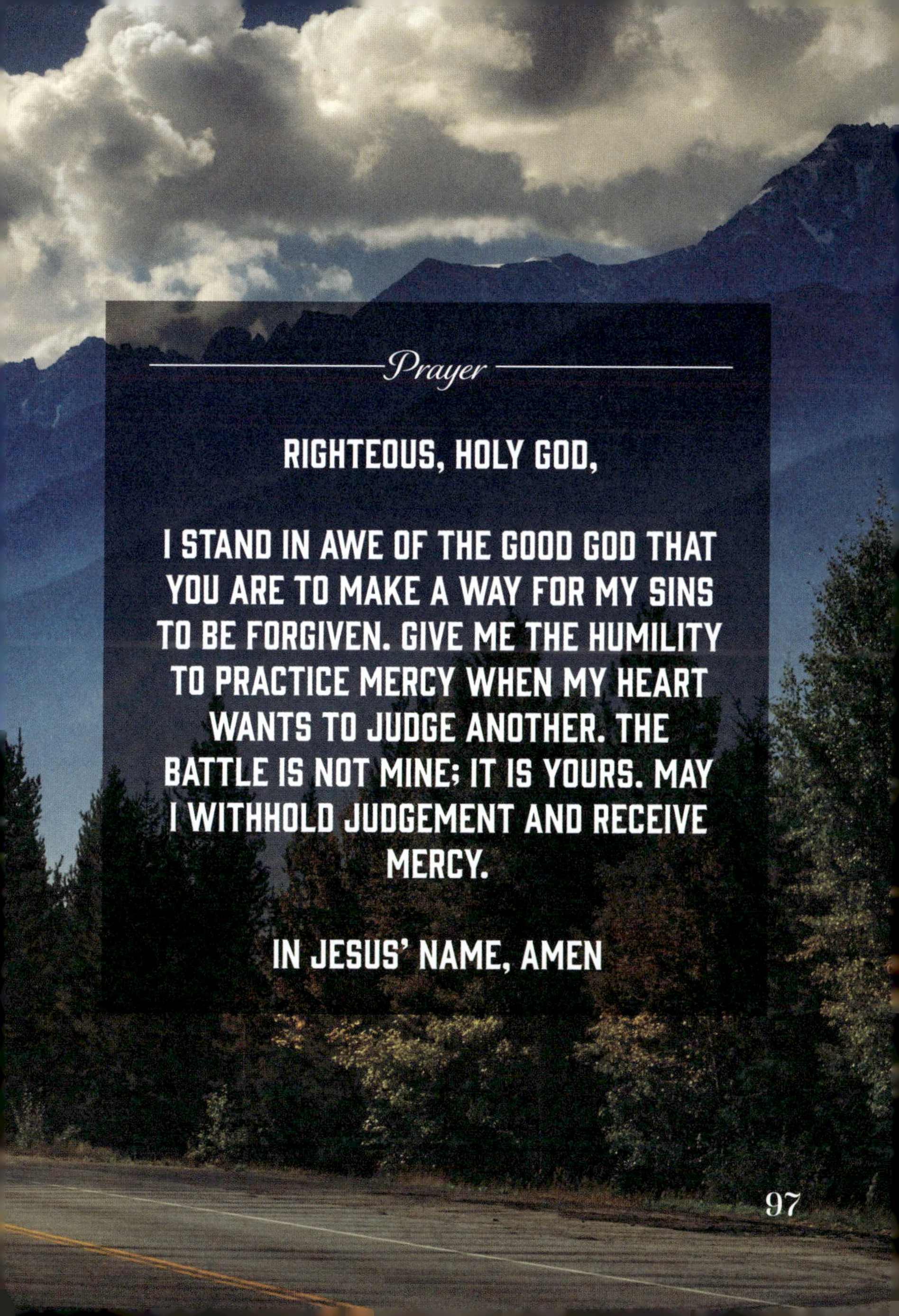

Prayer

RIGHTEOUS, HOLY GOD,

I STAND IN AWE OF THE GOOD GOD THAT YOU ARE TO MAKE A WAY FOR MY SINS TO BE FORGIVEN. GIVE ME THE HUMILITY TO PRACTICE MERCY WHEN MY HEART WANTS TO JUDGE ANOTHER. THE BATTLE IS NOT MINE; IT IS YOURS. MAY I WITHHOLD JUDGEMENT AND RECEIVE MERCY.

IN JESUS' NAME, AMEN

So then, each of us will give an account of ourselves to God. Therefore, let us stop passing judgment on one another. Instead, make up your mind not to put any stumbling block or obstacle in the way of a brother or sister.

ROMANS 14:12–13

Do not judge, and you will not be judged. Do not condemn, and you will not be condemned. Forgive, and you will be forgiven.

LUKE 6:37

Even fools are thought wise if they keep silent and discerning if they hold their tongues.

PROVERBS 17:28

Judgment will again be founded on righteousness, and all the upright in heart will follow it.

PSALMS 94:15

And I saw the dead, great and small, standing before the throne, and books were opened. Another book was opened, which is the book of life. The dead were judged according to what they had done as recorded in the books.

REVELATION 20:12

FIDELITY

Infidelity is one of the greatest causes for divorce in our nation. The enemy loves to tell men that they need more than their wife to be satisfied or that faithfulness is unnatural. Many men have been raised by fathers and influenced by uncles to be promiscuous before and after marriage. Remember, God loves his daughter more than you do and wants you to love her through faithful commitment physically, emotionally, and spiritually. Don't lose the gift of your "good thing" for something that looks good. It's not worth it.

Prayer

GOD,

I THANK YOU THAT YOU CREATED THE COVENANT OF MARRIAGE WITH ME IN MIND. YOU KNOW THAT ONE WOMAN IS ENOUGH FOR ME, ESPECIALLY WHEN I AM ALIGNED WITH YOU. TEACH ME TO TREAT MY WIFE LIKE THE GIFT THAT SHE IS TO ME. HELP ME TO RESIST THE TEMPTATION TO STEP OUTSIDE OF MY MARRIAGE SO I CAN BE IN RIGHT RELATIONSHIP WITH YOU AND MY WIFE.

AMEN

Enjoy life with your wife, whom you love, all the days of this meaningless life that God has given you under the sun—all your meaningless days. For this is your lot in life and in your toilsome labor under the sun.

ECCLESIASTES 9:9

In this same way, husbands ought to love their wives as their own bodies. He who loves his wife loves himself.

EPHESIANS 5:28

However, each one of you also must love his wife as he loves himself, and the wife must respect her husband.

EPHESIANS 5:33

A deacon must be faithful to his wife and must manage his children and his household well. Those who have served well gain an excellent standing and great assurance in their faith in Christ Jesus.

1 TIMOTHY 3:12–13

"I have the right to do anything," you say—but not everything is beneficial. "I have the right to do anything"—but I will not be mastered by anything.

1 CORINTHIANS 6:12

CONFLICT

As men, some of us thrive on conflict. We want to fight and win the battle, but if we're not wise we can lose the war. We are called to live at peace with people when it depends on us. Conflict is healthy because it is proof that different people are being honest about their feelings and beliefs. In the end, we have to handle conflict with grace and truth. Jesus didn't shy away from speaking truth to those in power or challenging those who dishonored the will of his father, but he did it in a way that honored the father. We can do the same.

Prayer

GOD,

BECAUSE I AM HUMAN, I KNOW THERE WILL BE CONFLICT IN MY LIFE. I CHOOSE TO REJECT PASSIVITY AND COMPLACENCY KNOWING THAT I AM SECURE IN WHO YOU'VE CREATED ME TO BE. HELP ME TO HANDLE CONFLICT WITH GRACE AND TRUTH SO THAT, IN THE END, I CAN HAVE PEACE WITH YOU AND OTHERS.

AMEN

Rescue me, LORD, from evildoers; protect me from the violent, who devise evil plans in their hearts and stir up war every day.

PSALMS 140:1–2

When a man's ways please the LORD, he maketh even his enemies to be at peace with him.

PROVERBS 16:7

Blessed are the peacemakers: for they shall be called the children of God.

MATTHEW 5:9

A hot-tempered person stirs up conflict, but the one who is patient calms a quarrel.

PROVERBS 15:18

"In your anger do not sin": Do not let the sun go down while you are still angry.

EPHESIANS 4:26

INTERCESSION

To intercede means to stand in the gap for another person. Jesus is the chief intercessor standing between us and God advocating for us before the father. In the same way, we are called to intercede for our families, our co-workers, and our communities. It doesn't matter who is in the White House, we should be praying for them in our house. We should pray for our children's future spouses and for our wives' purpose to be fulfilled. God has gifted us as leaders of our homes with the mantle of covering them with prayer knowing that he answers according to his way.

Prayer

FATHER,

FORGIVE ME FOR NOT INTERCEDING AS I SHOULD. I KNOW HOW IMPORTANT IT IS TO COVER MY FAMILY AND MY COMMUNITY IN PRAYER BECAUSE PRAYER CHANGES THINGS. I CHOOSE TO INTERCEDE FOR THE PEOPLE YOU PLACE ON MY HEART TODAY AND GOING FORWARD. I TRUST YOU TO MEET ME IN MOMENTS OF INTERCESSION.

AMEN

The LORD will fight for you; you need only to be still.

EXODUS 14:14

And I will ask the Father, and he will give you another advocate to help you and be with you forever.

JOHN 14:16

Who then is the one who condemns? No one. Christ Jesus who died—more than that, who was raised to life—is at the right hand of God and is also interceding for us.

ROMANS 8:34

But because Jesus lives forever, he has a permanent priesthood. Therefore, he is able to save completely those who come to God through him, because he always lives to intercede for them.

HEBREWS 7:24–25

I urge, then, first of all, that petitions, prayers, intercession and thanksgiving be made for all people—for kings and all those in authority, that we may live peaceful and quiet lives in all godliness and holiness.

1 TIMOTHY 2:1–2

REDEMPTION

There is nothing like getting a gift card for Father's Day to a place you really like whether it be a restaurant, clothing store, or golf course. There is a sense of freedom in knowing that your experience has already been paid for. The same is true in our relationship with God, our experience of abundant life on earth and eternal life in heaven has already been paid for, but we have to cash in. We have to take advantage of it. Live this day as if Jesus paid it all, because he did.

Prayer

JESUS,

THANK YOU FOR REDEEMING ME FROM THE PENALTY OF MY SINS. YOU SACRIFICED YOUR LIFE SO I COULD LIVE. I WANT TO CASH IN ON THE GIFT OF ABUNDANT LIFE TODAY KNOWING THAT IT'S COVERED IN YOUR BLOOD THAT WAS SHED ON CALVARY. THANK YOU FOR REDEEMING ME.

AMEN

And everyone who calls on the name of the Lord will be saved.

ACTS 2:21

Therefore, confess your sins to each other and pray for each other so that you may be healed. The prayer of a righteous person is powerful and effective.

JAMES 5:16

Be pleased to save me, LORD; come quickly, LORD, to help me.

PSALMS 40:13

For all have sinned and fall short of the glory of God, and all are justified freely by his grace through the redemption that came by Christ Jesus.

ROMANS 3:23–24

Do not let any unwholesome talk come out of your mouths, but only what is helpful for building others up according to their needs, that it may benefit those who listen. 30 And do not grieve the Holy Spirit of God, with whom you were sealed for the day of redemption.

EPHESIANS 4:29–30

HEALING

As men, we often struggle to go to the doctor or counseling because we don't want to admit we need help, or we don't want to know what is wrong with us. We often try to white knuckle our way to situations that ultimately lead to things getting worse. True healing starts with admitting we need it and then wanting to be healed. Jesus asked the man at the pool of Bethesda if he was comfortable being sick and when he responded that he wanted to be healed, Jesus healed him. May we seek help for our physical, emotional, and spiritual lives so we can be well for the purpose God has for us.

Prayer

JESUS,

WHAT AN AMAZING HEALER YOU ARE. YOU HEALED THE MAN BORN BLIND AND RAISED LAZARUS FROM THE DEAD. YOU RESTORED THE WOMAN WITH THE ISSUE OF BLOOD AND RAISED THE CENTURION'S DAUGHTER TO LIFE. MAY WELLNESS BE MY PORTION AND SEEKING HEALING BE MY POSTURE AS YOUR SON.

IN YOUR NAME, AMEN

"But I will restore you to health and heal your wounds," declares the LORD, "Because you are called an outcast, Zion for whom no one cares."

JEREMIAH 30:17

Worship the LORD your God, and his blessing will be on your food and water. I will take away sickness from among you.

EXODUS 23:25

Heal the sick who are there and tell them, 'The kingdom of God has come near to you.'

LUKE 10:9

He sent out his word and healed them; he rescued them from the grave.

PSALMS 107:20

When Jesus saw him lying there and knew that he had already been there a long time, he said to him, "Do you want to be healed?"

JOHN 5:6

SELF-CONTROL

Many strong men have been crippled under the weight of lack of self-control. Powerful men have lost self-control over women. Influential men have been weakened by greed or drunkenness. Try taking some time today to practice self-control in a simple way, like waiting to be the third person to share in a meeting or letting your wife finish her story without interrupting. See what a difference it will make today.

Prayer

JESUS,

AS YOU HUNG ON THE CROSS, YOU COULD HAVE EASILY WIELDED YOUR POWER TO DESTROY EVERY ROMAN SOLDIER AND MOCKER, BUT YOU PRACTICED SELF-CONTROL, PRAYING FOR THEIR FORGIVENESS. WHEN TEMPTED BY SATAN IN THE WILDERNESS AFTER 40 DAYS OF FASTING, YOU COULD HAVE EATEN THE BREAD, JUMPED FROM THE HIGH PLACE, OR ELEVATED YOURSELF, BUT YOU CHOSE SELF-CONTROL BY SUBMITTING TO YOUR FATHER. MAY I DO THE SAME IN MY LIFE TODAY.

AMEN

Blessed is the one who perseveres under trial because, having stood the test, that person will receive the crown of life that the Lord has promised to those who love him.

JAMES 1:12

You, however, must teach what is appropriate to sound doctrine. Teach the older men to be temperate, worthy of respect, self-controlled, and sound in faith, in love and in endurance.

TITUS 2:1–2

Like a city whose walls are broken through is a person who lacks self-control.

PROVERBS 25:28

But the fruit of the Spirit is love, joy, peace, patience, kindness, goodness, faithfulness, gentleness, self-control; against such things there is no law.

GALATIANS 5:22–23

For the grace of God has appeared that offers salvation to all people. It teaches us to say "No" to ungodliness and worldly passions, and to live self-controlled, upright and godly lives in this present age, while we wait for the blessed hope—the appearing of the glory of our great God and Savior, Jesus Christ, who gave himself for us to redeem us from all wickedness and to purify for himself a people that are his very own, eager to do what is good.

TITUS 2:11–14

PERSEVERANCE

Distance running is not for the faint of heart. Men who run marathons demonstrate a level of physical perseverance that many will never fully understand. In Scripture, the word perseverance means to remain under pressure without breaking. This is a skill learned under pressure. Often, God trusts us with pressure. Through it we learn that we can persevere. I've seen men persevere through sickness, pain, financial loss, and even the death of a child, in the power of the Spirit. You can persevere because the greater one lives in you.

Prayer

JESUS,

JUST AS YOU ENDURED THE FLOGGING AND CARRIED YOUR CROSS, HELP ME PERSEVERE THROUGH THE TRIALS THAT COME MY WAY. MAY I SEE THEM AS OPPORTUNITIES TO SEE HOW STRONG I AM IN YOU, AND HOW STRONG YOU CAN BE IN ME. GRANT ME PEACE AS I PERSEVERE IN YOU.

AMEN

So do not throw away your confidence; it will be richly rewarded. You need to persevere so that when you have done the will of God, you will receive what he has promised.

HEBREWS 10:35–36

And as for you, brothers and sisters, never tire of doing what is good.

2 THESSALONIANS 3:13

Let us not become weary in doing good, for at the proper time we will reap a harvest if we do not give up.

GALATIANS 6:9

Consider it pure joy, my brothers and sisters, whenever you face trials of many kinds, because you know that the testing of your faith produces perseverance. Let perseverance finish its work so that you may be mature and complete, not lacking anything.

JAMES 1:2–4

Therefore, since we are surrounded by such a great cloud of witnesses, let us throw off everything that hinders and the sin that so easily entangles. And let us run with perseverance the race marked out for us,

HEBREWS 12:1

OPEN-HEARTEDNESS

Our heavenly father is so generous. He has demonstrated his love for us in giving us his one and only son. He has given us spiritual gifts that can be used for the good of our community and for his glory. He has given us food to eat, clothes to wear, a place to live, and a purpose to live for. As his children, we can be generous as well demonstrating that we are his. You can't beat God in giving, so practice open-heartedness today and experience the gift that keeps on giving.

Prayer

FATHER,

THANK YOU FOR GIVING ME MORE THAN I DESERVE. YOU HAVE BEEN GRACIOUS TO ME. HELP ME TO BE OPEN-HEARTED, TO GIVE FROM WHAT YOU HAVE GIVEN ME, TRUSTING THAT YOU WILL PROVIDE ALL I NEED AND BLESS OTHERS THROUGH ME. WHAT A GIFT IT IS TO GIVE IN YOUR NAME. GLORIFY YOURSELF THROUGH ME.

IN JESUS' NAME, AMEN

Be kind and compassionate to one another, forgiving each other, just as in Christ God forgave you.

EPHESIANS 4:32

Remember this: Whoever sows sparingly will also reap sparingly, and whoever sows generously will also reap generously.

2 CORINTHIANS 9:6

And now these three remain: faith, hope and love. But the greatest of these is love.

1 CORINTHIANS 13:13

We have spoken freely to you, Corinthians, and opened wide our hearts to you.

2 CORINTHIANS 6:11

You will be enriched in every way so that you can be generous on every occasion, and through us your generosity will result in thanksgiving to God.

2 CORINTHIANS 9:11

SERVANTHOOD

The greatest man known to history was a servant first. Jesus Christ served the sick, imprisoned, demon-possesed, and even the dead. He was one who put others before himself. He served his way all the way to the cross. If the greatest man of all can serve, surely you as a man can serve God, your family, your church, and your community. Serving is a sign that you know God and he is known by you. As you serve, you grow to be more like him, the servant of all.

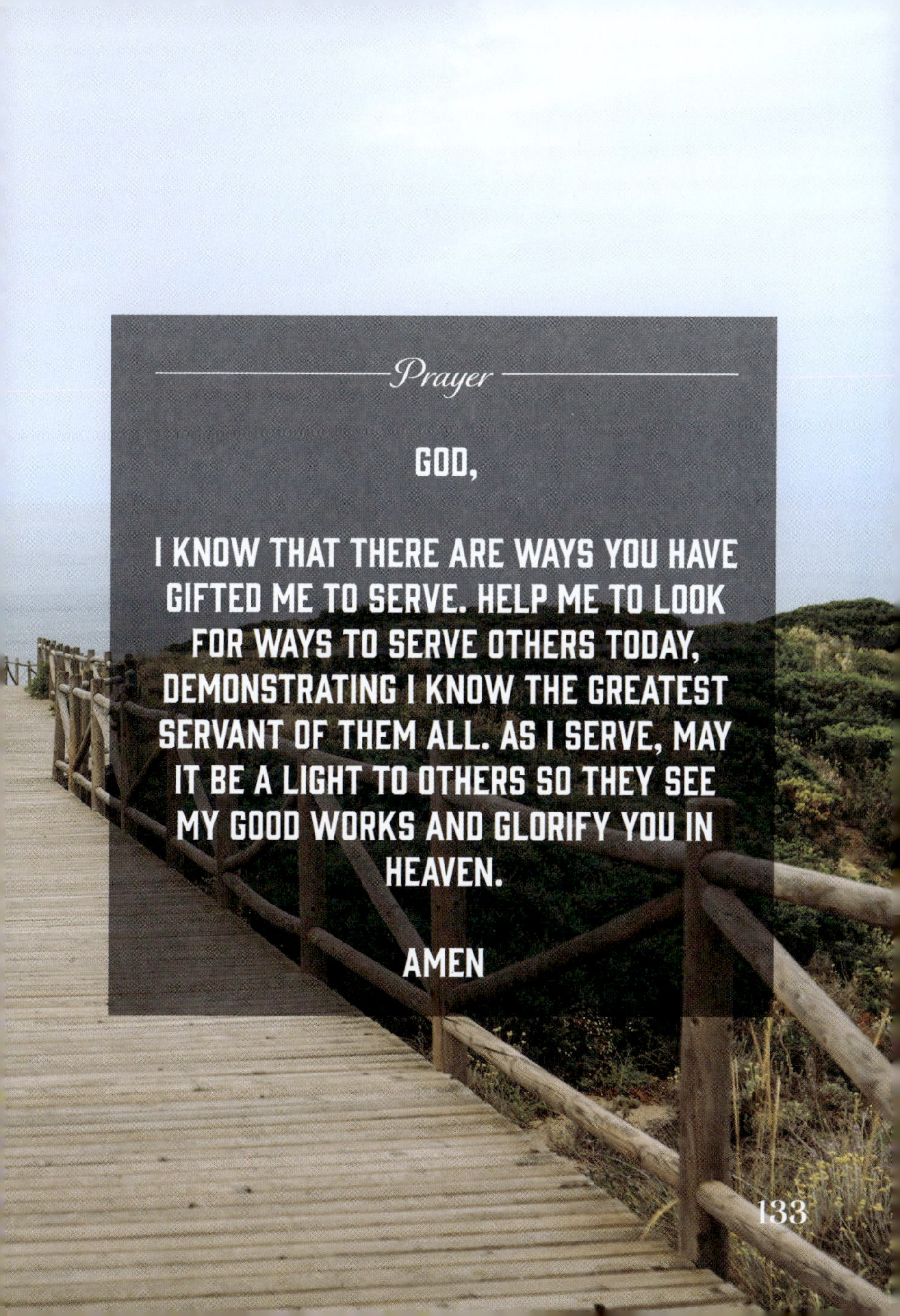

Prayer

GOD,

I KNOW THAT THERE ARE WAYS YOU HAVE GIFTED ME TO SERVE. HELP ME TO LOOK FOR WAYS TO SERVE OTHERS TODAY, DEMONSTRATING I KNOW THE GREATEST SERVANT OF THEM ALL. AS I SERVE, MAY IT BE A LIGHT TO OTHERS SO THEY SEE MY GOOD WORKS AND GLORIFY YOU IN HEAVEN.

AMEN

If they obey and serve him, they will spend the rest of their days in prosperity and their years in contentment.

JOB 36:11

Now all has been heard; here is the conclusion of the matter: Fear God and keep his commandments, for this is the duty of all mankind.

ECCLESIASTES 12:13

Now if you obey me fully and keep my covenant, then out of all nations you will be my treasured possession.

EXODUS 19:5

"Well done, my good servant!" his master replied. "Because you have been trustworthy in a very small matter, take charge of ten cities."

LUKE 19:17

You call me 'Teacher' and 'Lord,' and rightly so, for that is what I am. Now that I, your Lord and Teacher, have washed your feet, you also should wash one another's feet.

JOHN 13:13-14

ANXIETY

Anxiety seems to be the norm of our day. As men, we are anxious about providing for our families, making a difference in the world, and raising great kids. We are anxious about the news, the few who don't like us, and the challenges we see coming down the road. Anxiety can be a challenge if we don't choose to cast those anxieties on Christ. I encourage you to take your anxiety to him and allow him to give you peace in your heart and mind. He's up, so you might as well get some sleep.

Prayer

LORD,

I SEE MANY THINGS IN THIS WORLD THAT COULD MAKE MY HEART ANXIOUS. TODAY, I CHOOSE PEACE OVER MY PACING. I WILL TRUST THAT YOU WILL TAKE CARE OF EVERYONE OF MY NEEDS, KNOWING THAT YOU'RE A GOOD FATHER. I PUT MY COMPLETE TRUST IN YOU AND CHOOSE TO REMEMBER WHAT YOU'VE DONE AS A REMINDER OF WHAT YOU WILL DO IN THE FUTURE.

AMEN

Therefore, do not worry about tomorrow, for tomorrow will worry about itself. Each day has enough trouble of its own.

MATTHEW 6:34

So do not fear, for I am with you; do not be dismayed, for I am your God. I will strengthen you and help you; I will uphold you with my righteous right hand.

ISAIAH 41:10

God is our refuge and strength, an ever-present help in trouble. Therefore we will not fear, though the earth give way and the mountains fall into the heart of the sea, though its waters roar and foam and the mountains quake with their surging.

PSALMS 46: 1-3

Do not be anxious about anything, but in every situation, by prayer and petition, with thanksgiving, present your requests to God. And the peace of God, which transcends all understanding, will guard your hearts and your minds in Christ Jesus.

PHILIPPIANS 4:6–7

When anxiety was great within me, your consolations brought me joy.

PSALMS 94:19

COMFORT

All of us have needed comfort at some point on the journey called life. As boys, we needed comfort when we hurt ourselves playing on the playground. As adolescents, we needed comfort when we experienced our first heartbreak. As young men, we needed comfort when we weren't hired for a job. As grown men, we needed comfort when we lost a loved one close to our hearts. God is the God of all comfort. We can run to him when we need comfort and he will meet us there.

Prayer

HEAVENLY FATHER,

THERE ARE TIMES WHEN I DON'T FEEL I CAN TELL ANYONE ABOUT THE CHALLENGES I'M FACING. I FEEL LIKE I NEED TO BE STRONG FOR EVERYONE ELSE. I NEED YOU TO BE A STRONG TOWER FOR ME IN THIS MOMENT AND BRING COMFORT TO MY HEART. THANK YOU FOR BEING A COMFORTING GOD.

AMEN

When I am afraid, I put my trust in you.

PSALMS 56:3

For just as we share abundantly in the sufferings of Christ, so also our comfort abounds through Christ.

2 CORINTHIANS 1:5

Cast all your anxiety on him because he cares for you.

1 PETER 5:7

But my mouth would encourage you;
comfort from my lips would bring you
relief.

JOB 16:5

Praise be to the God and Father of
our Lord Jesus Christ, the Father of
compassion and the God of all comfort,
who comforts us in all our troubles, so
that we can comfort those in any trouble
with the comfort we ourselves receive
from God.

2 CORINTHIANS 1:3-4

DIVINE LOVE

Divine love is different from earthly love. Often as men, we are loved for what we can do for others, whether it's making money or protecting others from danger. But God's love is unconditional, with no strings attached. He loved us because he is love and we are his children. There is nothing my kids can do to make me love them more or make me love them less, and I am a human. So, we know that God's love surpasses any love we'll have on this earth. Brother, receive that love and give it to others freely.

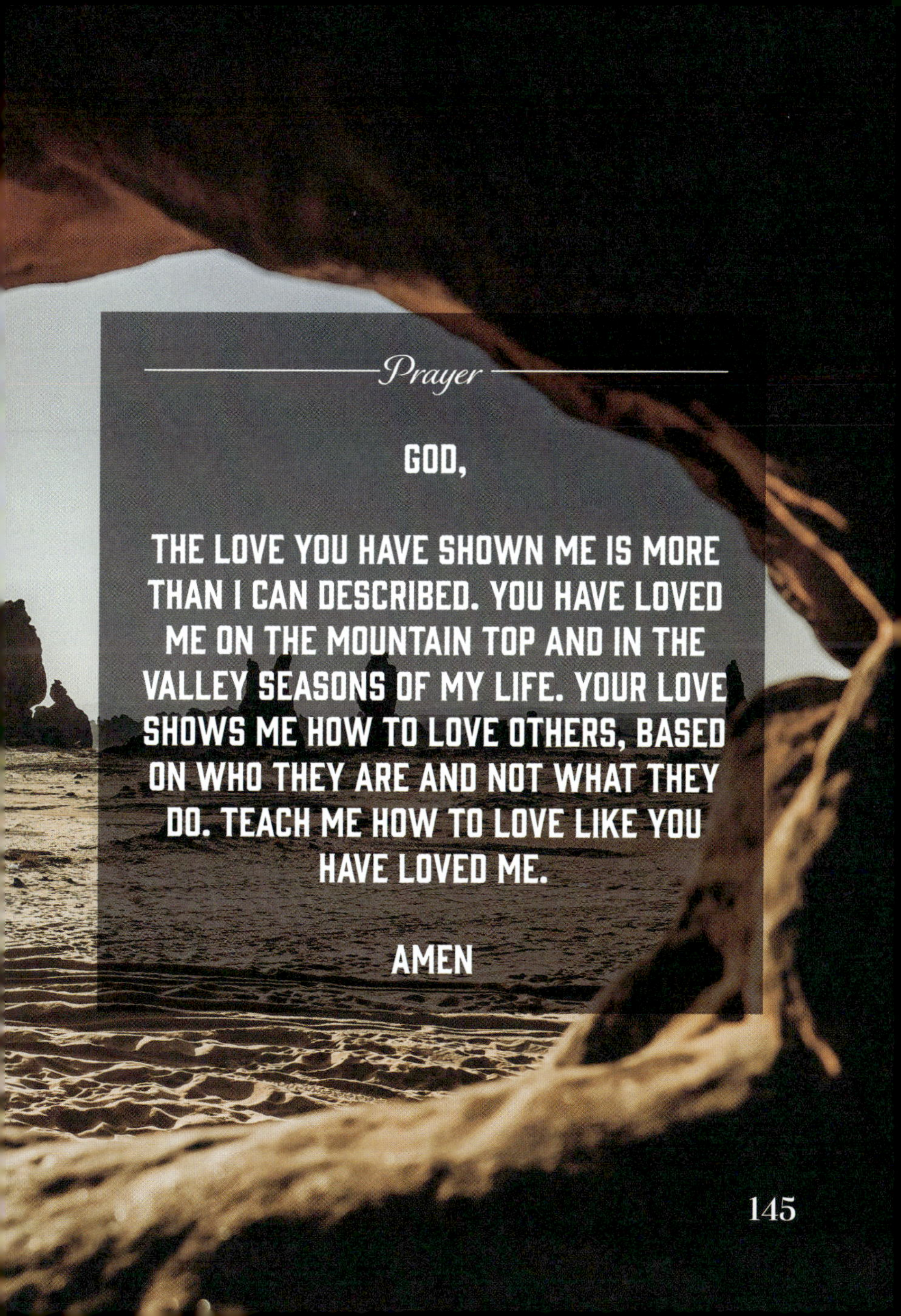

Prayer

GOD,

THE LOVE YOU HAVE SHOWN ME IS MORE THAN I CAN DESCRIBED. YOU HAVE LOVED ME ON THE MOUNTAIN TOP AND IN THE VALLEY SEASONS OF MY LIFE. YOUR LOVE SHOWS ME HOW TO LOVE OTHERS, BASED ON WHO THEY ARE AND NOT WHAT THEY DO. TEACH ME HOW TO LOVE LIKE YOU HAVE LOVED ME.

AMEN

I spread out my hands to you; I thirst for you like a parched land.

PSALMS 143:6

He said: "The LORD is my rock, my fortress and my deliverer; my God is my rock, in whom I take refuge, my shield and the horn of my salvation. He is my stronghold, my refuge and my savior—from violent people you save me."

2 SAMUEL 22:2–3

Give thanks to the LORD, for he is good; his love endures forever.

1 CHRONICLES 16:34

For the Lord is good; his steadfast love endures forever, and his faithfulness to all generations.

PSALMS 100:5

Dear friends, let us love one another, for love comes from God. Everyone who loves has been born of God and knows God.

1 JOHN 4:7

ACCEPTANCE

Often as teen boys, we struggled with finding acceptance from peers, parents, or romantic partners. We have insecurities as our voices change, our bodies grow, and our hormones rage. We try to make sense of it all, while often feeling unacceptable. Today, I am reminded that Jesus was baptized and was accepted by God without having performed any miracles or leading anyone back to God, yet. His acceptance was his superpower because he could live in security of his relationship with God.

Prayer

GOD,

I KNOW YOU DON'T ACCEPT EVERYTHING I DO, BECAUSE BEING HOLY, YOU CAN'T ACCEPT SIN. YET NO MATTER WHAT I DO, YOU ACCEPT ME, FOR WHO I AM. HELP ME TO ALIGN WHO I AM WITH WHO YOU CREATED ME TO BE, KNOWING THAT ACCEPTANCE IS ALREADY MINE THROUGH YOUR SON, JESUS. I ACCEPT YOUR GIFT OF ABUNDANT LIFE ANEW, TODAY.

AMEN

Do everything without grumbling or arguing.

PHILIPPIANS 2:14

Keep your lives free from the love of money and be content with what you have, because God has said, "Never will I leave you; never will I forsake you."

HEBREWS 13:5

Therefore, as you received Christ Jesus the Lord, so walk in him.

COLOSSIANS 2:6

And a voice from heaven said, "This is my Son, whom I love; with him I am well pleased."

MATTHEW 3:17

But the Lord said to Samuel, "Do not consider his appearance or his height, for I have rejected him. The Lord does not look at the things people look at. People look at the outward appearance, but the Lord looks at the heart."

1 SAMUEL 16:7

RESPONSIBILITY

All men are not equally capable. Some men are great with their hands while others are great with their mind. Some men can speak in front of crowds, while others share a few words. Some men are inspiring, while others are infuriating. One of the greatest abilities we can develop as men is responsibility. If we don't have it now, we can learn it through models and mentors. We can ask our heavenly father for the strength and fortitude to be more responsible. At the end of our lives, we want to have said, we did good work with what we've been given, but the rewards he gives will be worth it.

Prayer

LORD,

I REALIZE THAT WHEN YOU WERE GIVING OUT GIFTS, YOU DID NOT GIVE THEM EQUALLY, BUT YOU ASKED ME TO BE A GOOD STEWARD OF THE GIFTS YOU GAVE ME. HELP ME TO BE RESPONSIBLE WITH THE GIFTS AND ABILITIES I DO HAVE, WHILE CHOOSING TO GAIN NEW SKILLS BECAUSE YOU HAVE MADE ME A MAN WHO CAN CONTINUE TO GROW. I CHOOSE TO BE RESPONSIBLE TODAY.

AMEN

Anyone who does not provide for their relatives, and especially for their own household, has denied the faith and is worse than an unbeliever.

TIMOTHY 5:8

If anyone does not know how to manage his own family, how can he take care of God's church?

1 TIMOTHY 3:5

Let no debt remain outstanding, except the continuing debt to love one another, for whoever loves others has fulfilled the law.

ROMANS 13:8

No longer will they build houses and others live in them, or plant and others eat. For as the days of a tree, so will be the days of my people; my chosen ones will long enjoy the work of their hands.

ISAIAH 65:22

Look, I am coming soon! My reward is with me, and I will give to each person according to what they have done. I am the Alpha and the Omega, the First and the Last, the Beginning and the End.

REVELATION 22:12-13

MATURITY

The former toy company Toys R' Us was long known for its commercial jingle: "I don't want to grow up . . ." Sometimes, growing up is a struggle for men. During this season of our nation, we are seeing men struggle to launch in their early twenties, and struggle to maintain in their early thirties. Some grown men are playing childish games with the women in their lives and with God. It's time to grow up and be the man God has called you to be. Since you were born, you've grown physically. Take this opportunity to commit to growing in maturity so you're not deceived by the schemes of the enemy.

Prayer

JESUS,

YOU GREW IN STATURE AND IN FAVOR WITH GOD AND MEN. I WANT TO BE MORE LIKE YOU, WHERE MY PHYSICAL GROWTH ISN'T THE ONLY GROWTH, I EXPERIENCE. HELP ME TO MATURE TO MAKE EVEN BETTER DECISIONS, TRUSTING THAT YOU WILL REWARD MY FAITHFULNESS TO YOUR PURPOSE IN MY LIFE.

IN YOUR NAME, AMEN

Follow God's example, therefore, as dearly loved children.

EPHESIANS 5:1

When I was a child, I talked like a child, I thought like a child, I reasoned like a child. When I became a man, I put the ways of childhood behind me.

1 CORINTHIANS 13:11

Your wives, your children and your livestock may stay in the land that Moses gave you east of the Jordan, but all your fighting men, ready for battle, must cross over ahead of your fellow Israelites.

JOSHUA 1:14

Brothers and sisters, stop thinking like children. In regard to evil be infants, but in your thinking be adults.

1 CORINTHIANS 14:20

...until we all reach unity in the faith and in the knowledge of the Son of God and become mature, attaining to the whole measure of the fullness of Christ. Then we will no longer be infants, tossed back and forth by the waves, and blown here and there by every wind of teaching and by the cunning and craftiness of people in their deceitful scheming.

EPHESIANS 4:13–14

PEACE

Peace is one of the greatest commodities a man can have. When you have peace in your heart and your mind, you can be creative and productive. You can be an asset to others instead of a liability. Peace comes from knowing God through Jesus and keeping a short account with God. When we sin, confessing and repenting restores intimacy with God, the father. If you're struggling with peace today, consider if there is anything in your life you're holding on to, that God wants you to let go. Are you at peace with God? If so, ask him to help you walk at peace with yourself.

Prayer

JESUS,

BEFORE YOU WENT BACK TO YOUR HEAVENLY FATHER, YOU PROMISED ME PEACE THAT WAS DIFFERENT THAN THE WORLD'S DEFINITION OF PEACE. I WANT TO EXUDE PEACE IN MY HOME AND ON MY JOB. WHEN LIFE THROWS ME A CURVE BALL, I WANT TO KNOCK IT OUT OF MY MIND WITH THE PEACE YOU'VE GIVEN. I RECEIVE YOUR PEACE AS A GIFT YOU DIED TO GIVE ME. THANK YOU FOR YOUR PEACE.

AMEN

The LORD is my shepherd, I lack nothing. He makes me lie down in green pastures, he leads me beside quiet waters, he refreshes my soul. He guides me along the right paths for his name's sake. Even though I walk through the darkest valley, I will fear no evil, for you are with me; your rod and your staff, they comfort me.

PSALMS 23:1–4

If it is possible, as far as it depends on you, live at peace with everyone.

ROMANS 12:18

Submit to God and be at peace with him; in this way prosperity will come to you.

JOB 22:21

Therefore, tell him I am making my covenant of peace with him. He and his descendants will have a covenant of a lasting priesthood, because he was zealous for the honor of his God and made atonement for the Israelites.

NUMBERS 25:12–13

Peace I leave with you; my peace I give you. I do not give to you as the world gives. Do not let your hearts be troubled and do not be afraid.

JOHN 14:27

THE NEXT WORLD

Everybody wants to go to heaven, but few are in a hurry to get there. Jesus doesn't give us all the details about the next world, but he gives us a sneak preview, so we desire to experience the coming attraction. As men, we live in the tension of the now and the not yet. God's kingdom is coming and has already come. We live between the tension of the known world and the unknown next world. Heaven is a place prepared for prepared people. So, I encourage you to prepare as if you could go today and live as if you're already there.

Prayer

JESUS,

THANK YOU FOR THE PROMISE THAT YOU HAVE PREPARED A PLACE FOR ME IN YOUR FATHER'S HOUSE. I KNOW THAT HEAVEN IS FOR THOSE WHO HAVE CHOSEN A RELATIONSHIP WITH GOD THROUGH YOU. I PUT MY FAITH IN WHAT YOU HAVE DONE FOR ME AND LOOK FORWARD TO SPENDING ETERNITY WITH YOU AND ALL THOSE WHO HAVE DONE THE SAME. IN THE MEANTIME, HELP ME TO LIVE THE ABUNDANT LIFE YOU HAVE FOR ME TODAY.

AMEN

Jesus answered him, "Truly I tell you, today you will be with me in paradise."

LUKE 23:43

I will give you the keys of the kingdom of heaven, and whatever you bind on earth shall be bound in heaven, and whatever you loose on earth shall be loosed in heaven.

MATTHEW 16:19

Jesus answered, "My kingdom is not of this world. If my kingdom were of this world, my servants would have been fighting, that I might not be delivered over to the Jews. But my kingdom is not from the world."

JOHN 18:36

Do not let your hearts be troubled. You believe in God; believe also in me. My Father's house has many rooms; if that were not so, would I have told you that I am going there to prepare a place for you?

JOHN 14:1–2

See, I will create new heavens and a new earth. The former things will not be remembered, nor will they come to mind. But be glad and rejoice forever in what I will create, for I will create Jerusalem to be a delight and its people a joy.

ISAIAH 65:17–18

MISTAKES

Raising kids teaches you that mistakes happen all the time, whether it's a child tripping while trying to walk up the stairs or spilling juice while trying to pour it in a cup. We tend to have a great deal of grace for kids because we trust that they're growing. But when it comes to us as men, we struggle to give ourselves grace for the mistakes we make at work, at home, or in our church. God promises to uphold us with his hand. Making mistakes is human, making the same mistakes over and over again is immature. We have a choice to make when we make mistakes. I pray that we choose to grow from them instead of letting them defeat us.

Prayer

GOD,

I KNOW THAT I AM BOUND TO MAKE SOME MISTAKES AS I LIVE THIS LIFE TRYING TO HONOR YOU. I PRAY THAT YOU GIVE ME THE GRACE TO HANDLE THE MISTAKES I MAKE AND TO LEARN FROM THEM, SO I DON'T HAVE TO MAKE THE SAME MISTAKES AGAIN. KEEP ME GROUNDED IN YOUR LOVE FOR ME AS YOUR SON AND HELP ME KNOW THAT YOU'RE CHEERING ME ON IN MY GROWTH IN YOU.

IN JESUS' NAME, AMEN

When I said, “My foot is slipping,” your unfailing love, LORD, supported me.

PSALMS 94:18

Though he may stumble, he will not fall, for the LORD upholds him with his hand.

PSALMS 37:24

The Lord upholds all who are falling and raises up all who are bowed down.

PSALMS 145:14

It is better not to make a vow than to make one and not fulfill it. Do not let your mouth lead you into sin. And do not protest to the temple messenger, "My vow was a mistake." Why should God be angry at what you say and destroy the work of your hands?

ECCLESIASTES 5:5–6

Remnant of Judah, the Lord has told you, 'Do not go to Egypt.' Be sure of this: I warn you today that you made a fatal mistake when you sent me to the Lord your God and said, 'Pray to the Lord our God for us; tell us everything he says and we will do it.'

JEREMIAH 42:19–20

INTEGRITY

Who are you when no one is looking? This is a question that we as men need to ask ourselves on a daily basis. As godly men, we are called to integrity, which is living with a sameness between our public lives and private lives. The more we can have congruence between these two, the more honorable our lives can become. Daily we get to choose how we will live. I encourage you to choose integrity over duplicity today.

Prayer

GOD,

AT TIMES I MAY STRUGGLE WITH INTEGRITY BECAUSE I FEAR REJECTION. I AM AFRAID THAT PEOPLE WON'T ACCEPT ME FOR WHO I AM. AT OTHER TIMES I STRUGGLE WITH INTEGRITY BECAUSE I DON'T WANT TO LIVE UP TO THE STANDARDS YOU HAVE FOR ME. HELP ME TO LIVE A LIFE THAT IS INTEGROUS, BRINGING GLORY TO YOUR NAME AND SECURITY TO THOSE IN MY LIFE.

AMEN

Better the poor whose walk is blameless than a fool whose lips are perverse.

PROVERBS 19:1

Teach me to do your will, for you are my God; may your good Spirit lead me on level ground.

PSALMS 143:10

When a man makes a vow to the LORD or takes an oath to obligate himself by a pledge, he must not break his word but must do everything he said.

NUMBERS 30:2

Better is one day in your courts than a thousand elsewhere; I would rather be a doorkeeper in the house of my God than dwell in the tents of the wicked.

PSALMS 84:10

Righteousness guards the person of integrity, but wickedness overthrows the sinner.

PROVERBS 13:6

SELFLESSNESS

Jesus is the perfect example of a man who lived a selfless life when he didn't have to. In his glory and power, he could have selfishly stayed heaven with the father. Yet, he chose to practice selflessness for us. When he could have walked away from facing the cross in Gethsemane, he surrendered and said, not *my* will but *your* will be done. As you go throughout today, think about the ways you can lay your life down, the way Jesus laid his life down for you.

Prayer

JESUS,

THANK YOU FOR BEING A SELFLESS SAVIOR AND LEADER. YOUR MODEL INSPIRES ME TO LIVE MY LIFE SELFLESSLY AS WELL. GIVE ME THE STRENGTH AND WISDOM TO WALK OUT SERVING OTHERS THROUGHOUT THIS DAY.

IN YOUR NAME, AMEN

We who are strong ought to bear with the failings of the weak and not to please ourselves.

ROMANS 15:1

Give to everyone who asks you, and if anyone takes what belongs to you, do not demand it back. Do to others as you would have them do to you.

LUKE 6:30–31

Now that I, your Lord and Teacher, have washed your feet, you also should wash one another's feet.

JOHN 13:14

This is how we know what love is: Jesus Christ laid down his life for us. And we ought to lay down our lives for our brothers and sisters.

1 JOHN 3:16

Going a little farther, he fell with his face to the ground and prayed, "My Father, if it is possible, may this cup be taken from me. Yet not as I will, but as you will."

MATTHEW 26:39

LOVE

Jesus knew that love would be the difference between his true followers and the religious leaders of the day. As men, we often communicate our love for our favorite sports team or for our favorite food, but we have an opportunity to live out the unconditional love that Christ came to give. We can demonstrate love to our spouse or children which is easier because they're family, but we also get to demonstrate love to our neighbors or even our enemies. How will you live out love today?

Prayer

GOD,

YOU ARE LOVE. YOU DEMONSTRATED YOUR LOVE BY SENDING YOUR SON JESUS TO DIE FOR MY SINS. THANK YOU FOR LOVING ME. THANK YOU FOR YOUR SACRIFICE FOR ME. HELP ME TO LOVE OTHERS THE WAY YOU HAVE LOVED ME, UNCONDITIONALLY.

IN JESUS' NAME, AMEN

There is no fear in love. But perfect love drives out fear, because fear has to do with punishment. The one who fears is not made perfect in love.

1 JOHN 4:18

It always protects, always trusts, always hopes, always perseveres.

1 CORINTHIANS 13:7

Hatred stirs up conflict, but love covers over all wrongs.

PROVERBS 10:12

Above all, love each other deeply, because love covers over a multitude of sins.

PETER 4:8

We love because he loved us first.

1 JOHN 4:19

SHARING THE WORD

As a father, I often am asked if I am going to do what I promised my daughters I'd do. I often say, "Take my word for it." My word means something to them because I keep my promises. The same is true with God, he is inviting us to share his word with others so they can meet the God that keeps his promises. So many men have felt let down by God, their church, or even other believers. The more we share the word, the more we remind them that we serve a promise keeping God.

Prayer

JESUS,

YOU ARE THE WORD THAT BECAME FLESH AND DWELLED WITH US. I KNOW THAT THOUGH SHARING YOUR WORD WITH OTHERS, I CAN MAKE YOU KNOWN TO OTHER MEN WHO NEED TO KNOW YOU. GIVE ME EYES TO SEE THE MEN AROUND ME WHO WILL RECEIVE YOUR WORD. MAY I BE FAITHFUL TO SHARE YOUR WORD WITH THEM TODAY.

IN YOUR NAME, AMEN

I will give thanks to you, LORD, with all my heart; I will tell of all your wonderful deeds.

PSALMS 9:1

These commandments that I give you today are to be on your hearts. Impress them on your children. Talk about them when you sit at home and when you walk along the road, when you lie down and when you get up.

DEUTERONOMY 6:6–7

In the beginning was the Word, and the Word was with God, and the Word was God.

JOHN 1:1

Sing to the LORD, all the earth; proclaim his salvation day after day. Declare his glory among the nations, his marvelous deeds among all peoples.

1 CHRONICLES 16:23–24

In the same way, let your light shine before others, so that they may see your good works and give glory to your Father who is in heaven.

MATTHEW 5:16

ENVY

As boys, we grow up comparing ourselves to other boys. We're checking to see if another boy is stronger, faster, taller, or smarter. As we grow into men, we often compare cars, houses, accomplishments, and families. It is easy to envy others who have more than you have or are living a life that seems better than yours. With the rise of social media, we have more opportunities to envy than ever before. Our opportunity is to practice gratitude instead of envy, knowing that envy leads to destructive decisions.

Prayer

GOD,

I WANT TO BE GRATEFUL FOR ALL YOU HAVE DONE FOR ME. I WANT TO BE CONTENT WITH WHERE I AM WHILE CONTINUING TO GROW INTO WHO YOU'VE CALLED ME TO BE. HELP ME NOT GET DISTRACTED BY ENVYING OTHERS THAT HAVE BEEN BLESSED WITH THINGS I DESIRE. MAY I PRAISE YOU FOR THE GOOD YOU'VE DONE IN THEIR LIVES AND TRUST YOU IN THE MOMENT.

AMEN

Then he said to them, “Watch out! Be on your guard against all kinds of greed; life does not consist in an abundance of possessions.”

LUKE 12:15

For the love of money is a root of all kinds of evil. Some people, eager for money, have wandered from the faith and pierced themselves with many griefs.

1 TIMOTHY 6:10

Therefore, rid yourselves of all malice, deceit, hypocrisy, envy, and slander of every kind.

1 PETER 2:1

You shall not covet your neighbor's house; you shall not covet your neighbor's wife, or his male servant, or his female servant, or his ox, or his donkey, or anything that is your neighbor's.

EXODUS 20:17

Do not fret because of those who are evil or be envious of those who do wrong.

PSALMS 37:1

STRENGTH

Do you remember when you first lifted weights in the gym as a teenager? It was so exhilarating to see your muscles grow as the testosterone began to do its job. Being strong makes you feel safe, secure, and empowered. Growing into manhood often leads you to present as strong when you're struggling or feeling weak. The gift of our weakness is the strength of our savior. May your strength be found in Christ and what he has done for you and may you allow his strength to be made perfect in your weakness.

Prayer

JESUS,

YOU ARE THE STRONGEST FORCE THE WORLD HAS SEEN, YET YOU USED YOUR STRENGTH TO BLESS OTHERS. YOU CHOSE NOT TO DEMEAN OR DISMISS THOSE WHO WERE WEAKER THAN YOU. HELP ME TO USE MY STRENGTH IN WAYS THAT ADD VALUE TO OTHERS.

IN YOUR NAME, AMEN

But those who hope in the LORD will renew their strength. They will soar on wings like eagles; they will run and not grow weary, they will walk and not be faint.

ISAIAH 40:31

But he said to me, "My grace is sufficient for you, for my power is made perfect in weakness." Therefore, I will boast all the more gladly about my weaknesses, so that Christ's power may rest on me.

2 CORINTHIANS 12:9

Just before dawn Paul urged them all to eat. "For the last fourteen days," he said, "you have been in constant suspense and have gone without food—you haven't eaten anything."

ACTS 27:33

They go from strength to strength; each one appears before God in Zion

PSALMS 84:7

Finally, be strong in the Lord and in his mighty power.

EPHESIANS 6:10

BELIEF

It's one thing to believe God exists, it's another thing to believe in him. Many men recognize there is a higher power, but they haven't put their belief in him. When we believe in Jesus, we're saying we believe he lived a perfect life, died on the cross, and rose from the dead in our place for our sins. Daily, we need to believe in Christ afresh, knowing that circumstances can lead to seeds of doubt being planted in our hearts. Let's believe God consistently knowing that he has proven that he is trustworthy.

Prayer

GOD,

THANK YOU FOR GIVING ME THE FAITH TO BELIEVE ON YOU AS THE SCRIPTURE SAYS. I ACKNOWLEDGE THAT THERE ARE DAYS WHEN MY BELIEF BEGINS TO WANE AND I STRUGGLE TO BELIEVE. I INVITE YOU TO INFUSE MY HEART WITH FAITH TO BELIEVE YOU BASED ON YOUR WORD KNOWING THAT YOU'RE A GOOD FATHER.

AMEN

Do not be afraid of what you are about to suffer. I tell you, the devil will put some of you in prison to test you, and you will suffer persecution for ten days. Be faithful, even to the point of death, and I will give you life as your victor's crown.

REVELATION 2:10

They replied, "Believe in the Lord Jesus, and you will be saved—you and your household."

ACTS 16:31

So we fix our eyes not on what is seen, but on what is unseen, since what is seen is temporary, but what is unseen is eternal.

2 CORINTHIANS 4:18

If you declare with your mouth, "Jesus is Lord," and believe in your heart that God raised him from the dead, you will be saved.

ROMANS 10:9

Immediately the boy's father exclaimed, "I do believe; help me overcome my unbelief!"

MARK 9:24

WISDOM

As men, we love to show how smart we can be, but the value we bring to the table is more demonstrated through wisdom. Knowing what to do and being able to do it are two different things. My hope is that you will seek wisdom from those who are older than you and gain wisdom from the experiences you've had in life. Thankfully, we serve a God who gives wisdom liberally to us when we ask. So, I encourage you to ask for wisdom today for even the smallest things because God is there to give it.

Prayer

GOD,

THANK YOU FOR THE WAYS YOU'VE GIVEN ME THE WISDOM I'VE HAD IN THE PAST. HELP NOT TO TAKE THAT FOR GRANTED AND CONTINUE TO ASK FOR WISDOM DAILY. YOU ARE SO FAITHFUL TO PROVIDE WISDOM AS I AM WILLING TO ASK. I TRUST YOU TO BE THE ALL-WISE GOD I READ ABOUT IN SCRIPTURE.

AMEN

My son, if your heart is wise, then my heart will be glad indeed.

PROVERBS 23:15

Gold there is, and rubies in abundance, but lips that speak knowledge are a rare jewel.

PROVERBS 20:15

The fear of the LORD is the beginning of knowledge: but fools despise wisdom and instruction.

PROVERBS 1:7

If any of you lacks wisdom, let him ask God, who gives generously to all without reproach, and it will be given him.

JAMES 1:5

In him we have redemption through his blood, the forgiveness of sins, in accordance with the riches of God's grace that he lavished on us.

EPHESIANS 1:7–8

MIRACLES

As men, we tend to be logical and focused on facts instead of being mystical and focused on feelings. This reality causes us to struggle to believe things that we cannot explain. If we can't make it make sense through our education or experience, we struggle to believe. Jesus calls us to understand that with him all things are possible. He can heal those who are sick and even raise the dead. He can bring the resources to meet your needs. Trust him to do a miracle in your life even today.

Prayer

JESUS,

I HAVE READ OF THE MIRACLES YOU DID WHILE YOU WERE HERE ON EARTH. I REALIZE THAT IT SEEMS LIKE THIS ISN'T AS TYPICAL AS IT WAS THEN, BUT I STILL WANT TO BELIEVE YOU CAN DO SOMETHING I CANNOT EXPLAIN. I TRUST YOU TO BE A MIRACLE-WORKING GOD WHO DOES THE IMPOSSIBLE. THE FACT THAT I KNOW YOU AND HAVEN'T SEEN YOU IS ONE EXAMPLE THAT I CAN LOOK TO DAILY. THANK YOU FOR THE MIRACLE OF SALVATION.

AMEN

Taking the five loaves and the two fish and looking up to heaven, he gave thanks and broke them. Then he gave them to the disciples to distribute to the people. They all ate and were satisfied, and the disciples picked up twelve basketfuls of broken pieces that were left over.

LUKE 9:16–17

Just then a woman who had been subject to bleeding for twelve years came up behind him and touched the edge of his cloak. She said to herself, "If I only touch his cloak, I will be healed. Jesus turned and saw her. "Take heart, daughter," he said, "your faith has healed you." And the woman was healed at that moment.

MATTHEW 9:20–2

I am the LORD, the God of all mankind. Is anything too hard for me?

JEREMIAH 32:27

Simon's mother-in-law was in bed with a fever, and they immediately told Jesus about her. So, he went to her, took her hand and helped her up. The fever left her and she began to wait on them.

MARK 1:30-31

But I want you to know that the Son of Man has authority on earth to forgive sins. So, he said to the paralyzed man, "Get up, take your mat and go home."

MATTHEW 9:6

GOOD WORKS

Why would good works be so important to a godly man? After all, we know that salvation is not by works but by faith. Good works express the gratitude of the man who has been reconciled to God. It is the evidence of the love of God and appreciation for His greatest creation, mankind. It is the fruit of our spiritual maturity, when we prioritize doing good to our fellow man as our habit. When we see a need, we do the work to meet it in love and wisdom. Jesus said that what do it to the least of these, we do it unto him.

Prayer

LORD,

I THANK YOU FOR THE OPPORTUNITIES YOU PROVIDE FOR MY TALENTS, TIME, AND TREASURE TO MANIFEST GOOD WORKS THAT GLORIFY YOUR NAME. HELP ME SUBMIT TO THE GUIDANCE OF THE HOLY SPIRIT, TO SEE THE NEEDS AROUND ME, AND TO DO GOOD WORKS THAT BRING GLORY AND HONOR TO YOUR NAME. MAY MY GOOD WORKS DRAW THE LOST, HELP THE NEEDY, AND SHOW HOSPITALITY TO THE HOUSEHOLD OF FAITH.

IN JESUS' NAME, AMEN

The King will reply, “Truly I tell you, whatever you did for one of the least of these brothers and sisters of mine, you did for me.”

MATTHEW 25:40

You see that a person is considered righteous by what they do and not by faith alone.

JAMES 2:24

And let us consider how we may spur one another on toward love and good deeds.

HEBREWS 10:24

And we know that for those who love God all things work together for good, for those who are called according to his purpose.

ROMANS 8:28

Our people must learn to devote themselves to doing what is good, in order to provide for urgent needs and not live unproductive lives.

TITUS 3:14

MERCY

Mercy is a gift of grace that we don't deserve. At times, we can be judgmental of others, lacking the empathy needed to relate to their situation. I've learned that the more mercy I receive from others, the more mercy I am open to giving. I am grateful that Jesus was a man of mercy and gives me an opportunity to model my life after him to give mercy to others. I challenge you to extend mercy to the people in your life and see the fruit that it produces.

Prayer

LORD,

THANK YOU FOR THE MERCY YOU'VE EXTENDED TO ME. THERE ARE TIMES WHERE I STRUGGLE TO BE MERCIFUL TO OTHERS. I REALIZE THAT THIS IS NOT A TRAIT I WANT TO HAVE. HELP ME TO EXTEND MERCY TO MY FRIENDS, FAMILY, AND EVEN MY ENEMIES. I KNOW THAT'S WHAT YOU WOULD DO. THOUGH MANY MAY NOT SEE IT AS A MANLY CHOICE, I SEE IT AS A CHANCE TO BE MORE LIKE YOU. I TRUST YOU TO HELP ME IN THIS WAY.

IN JESUS' NAME, AMEN

And he passed in front of Moses, proclaiming, "The LORD, the LORD, the compassionate and gracious God, slow to anger, abounding in love and faithfulness."

EXODUS 34:6

Those who are kind benefit themselves, but the cruel bring ruin on themselves.

PROVERBS 11:17

Give thanks to the LORD, for he is good; his love endures forever.

1 CHRONICLES 16:34

For the Lord your God is a merciful God; he will not abandon or destroy you or forget the covenant with your ancestors, which he confirmed to them by oath.

DEUTERONOMY 4:31

Hear, Lord, and be merciful to me; Lord, be my help.

PSALMS 30:10

BRAVERY

One of the traits I love about my father is his bravery. He served 20 years in the military and fought in Vietnam. Yet, his biggest bravery demonstrated was his ability to submit to Christ as his Savior. After growing up in the church, he had a real encounter with God that transformed him. He became a pastor and community leader inspiring so many people. I think the bravest choice we as men can make is to submit to Christ as our savior and leader.

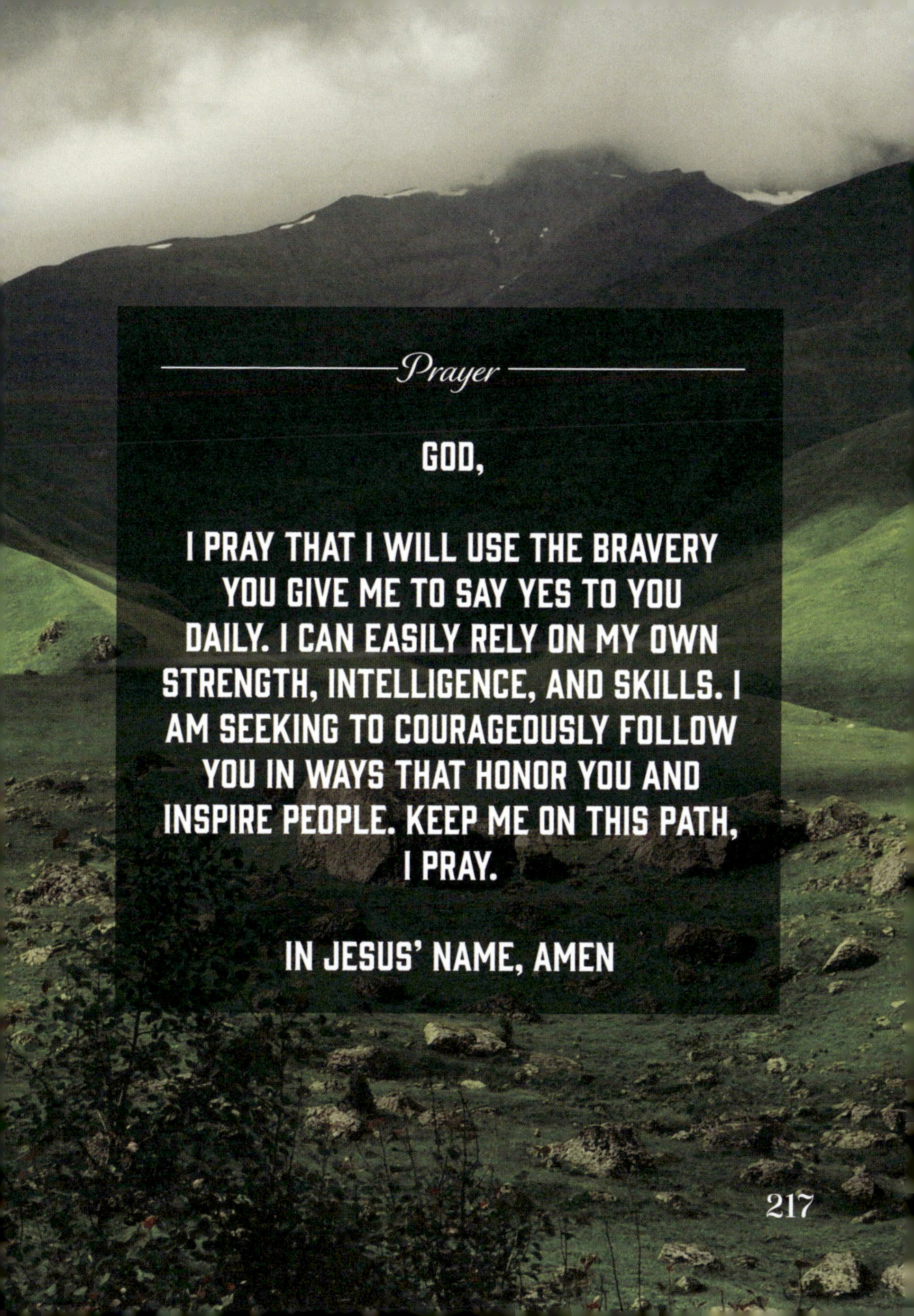

Prayer

GOD,

I PRAY THAT I WILL USE THE BRAVERY YOU GIVE ME TO SAY YES TO YOU DAILY. I CAN EASILY RELY ON MY OWN STRENGTH, INTELLIGENCE, AND SKILLS. I AM SEEKING TO COURAGEOUSLY FOLLOW YOU IN WAYS THAT HONOR YOU AND INSPIRE PEOPLE. KEEP ME ON THIS PATH, I PRAY.

IN JESUS' NAME, AMEN

You will not fear the terror of night, nor the arrow that flies by day, nor the pestilence that stalks in the darkness, nor the plague that destroys at midday. A thousand may fall at your side, ten thousand at your right hand, but it will not come near you.

PSALMS 91:5–7

Be strong and very courageous. Be careful to obey all the law my servant Moses gave you; do not turn from it to the right or to the left, that you may be successful wherever you go

JOSHUA 1:7

Rise up; this matter is in your hands. We will support you, so take courage and do it.

EZRA 10:4

Saul said to David, "Here is my older daughter Merab. I will give her to you in marriage; only serve me bravely and fight the battles of the Lord." For Saul said to himself, "I will not raise a hand against him. Let the Philistines do that!"

1 SAMUEL 18:17

David summoned all the officials of Israel to assemble at Jerusalem: the officers over the tribes, the commanders of the divisions in the service of the king, the commanders of thousands and commanders of hundreds, and the officials in charge of all the property and livestock belonging to the king and his sons, together with the palace officials, the warriors and all the brave fighting men.

1 CHRONICLES 28:1

BROTHERHOOD

I grew up with one brother and wanted sisters. As I've grown, I've come to have friends who are like brothers to me. There is nothing like connecting with other men who are going through similar challenges and successes. Men get men. We understand the challenges that come with carrying our burdens and they get how focused we can be on our work. Men understand us and will give us the benefit of the doubt. If you're lacking brotherhood, I challenge you to see brothers who have your values and can encourage you to be the best you can be.

Prayer

GOD,

YOU CHOSE TO LIVE AS A COMMUNITY AS THE FATHER, SON, AND HOLY SPIRIT. YOU REMINDED US THAT IT IS NOT GOOD FOR US TO BE ALONE. I PRAY THAT YOU WILL HELP ME APPRECIATE THE BROTHERS YOU HAVE PLACED IN MY LIFE AND SEEK RELATIONSHIPS WITH GODLY MEN WHO CAN HELP GROW INTO ALL YOU'VE CALLED ME TO BE.

IN JESUS' NAME, AMEN

A brother wronged is more unyielding than a fortified city; disputes are like the barred gates of a citadel.

PROVERBS 18:19

Be devoted to one another in love. Honor one another above yourselves.

ROMANS 12:10

How good and pleasant it is when God's people live together in unity!

PSALMS 133:1

A friend loves at all times, and a brother is born for adversity.

PROVERBS 17:17

Then Peter came to Jesus and asked, "Lord, how many times shall I forgive my brother or sister who sins against me? Up to seven times?" Jesus answered, "I tell you, not seven times, but seventy-seven times."

MATTHEW 18:21–22

FORGIVENESS

How are you when it comes to forgiveness? Are you quick to forgive or do you feel the need to keep retelling the story and hold a grudge. As a man of God, we are called to forgive because we have been forgiven. If you struggle to forgive, ask yourself the question, why? What makes you feel that you should hold a grudge when Christ has forgiven you? I invite you to consider this truth and seek to forgive. It will bless you even more than the person you're forgiving.

Prayer

GOD,

I KNOW YOU HAVE FORGIVEN ME OF ALL MY SINS PAST, PRESENT, AND FUTURE. I KNOW THAT UNFORGIVENESS CAN LEAD TO BITTERNESS AND I DON'T WANT TO BE BITTER. I ALSO KNOW THAT UNFORGIVENESS CAN LEAD TO HINDERED PRAYERS. HELP ME TO BE QUICK TO FORGIVE KNOWING THAT THIS IS YOUR HEART. I ASK THIS IN THE POWERFUL NAME OF JESUS.

AMEN

If we confess our sins, he is faithful and just to forgive us our sins, and to cleanse us from all unrighteousness.

1 JOHN 1:9

The Lord our God is merciful and forgiving, even though we have rebelled against him.

DANIEL 9:9

Therefore, I tell you, her sins, which are many, are forgiven—for she loved much. But he who is forgiven little, loves little.

LUKE 7:47

And when you stand praying, if you hold anything against anyone, forgive them, so that your Father in heaven may forgive you your sins.

MARK 11:25

For I will forgive their wickedness and will remember their sins no more.

HEBREWS 8:12

A GODLY LIFE

My brother, I pray that you are realizing the benefits of living the godly life. When you choose to live a godly life, you not only avoid the natural consequences of sin, but the spiritual consequences of less intimacy with our heavenly father. We know that God forgives us of our sins when we confess, but he doesn't release us from all of the consequences. Until we confess, the intimacy is impacted greatly. I pray you never lose your sensitivity to the Holy Spirit, who convicts us of sin and calls us to a godly life.

Prayer

GOD,

I KNOW THAT HUMAN PERFECTION IS NOT POSSIBLE FOR ME, BUT I CAN CHOOSE TO LIVE A GODLY LIFE. I WANT TO BE A MAN OF INTEGRITY WHO LIVES A LIFE THAT IS CHARACTERIZED BY YOUR CHARACTER. KEEP ME FROM FALLING INTO SIN PATTERNS THAT KEEP ME FROM BEING AN AMBASSADOR FOR YOU. HELP ME TO QUICKLY REPENT WHEN I SIN, KNOWING THAT YOU FORGIVE FREELY.

AMEN

Jesus answered, “I am the way and the truth and the life. No one comes to the Father except through me.”

JOHN 14:6

Do not conform to the pattern of this world but be transformed by the renewing of your mind. Then you will be able to test and approve what God’s will is—his good, pleasing and perfect will.

ROMANS 12:2

So, I say, walk by the Spirit, and you will not gratify the desires of the flesh.

GALATIANS 5:16

Whoever has the Son has life; whoever does not have the Son of God does not have life.

1 JOHN 5:12

But godliness with contentment is great gain.

1 TIMOTHY 6:6

TRUST

If you are a man with a decent job and some benefits, it is easy not to trust in God because you have options. If you get sick, you can go to the doctor. If you have a financial challenge, you can get a loan or use a credit card. Many around the world don't have those choices and then tend to trust God more. Have you ever thought about how much you do in life without God? If I'm honest, I know it can be more than I think. The good news is that our God is trustworthy and so we can daily choose to put our trust in him.

Prayer

HEAVENLY FATHER,

THANK YOU FOR ALLOWING ME TO PUT MY TRUST IN YOU FOR MY SALVATION. THAT CHOICE HAS CHANGED MY LIFE AND GIVEN ME CONFIDENCE THAT I HAVE ETERNAL LIFE SECURED WITH YOU. I AM ASKING THAT I WOULD TRUST YOU FOR THE DAILY NEEDS I HAVE, KNOWING THAT YOU ARE TRUSTWORTHY TO PROVIDE FOR ME. I LOOK FORWARD TO TRUSTING YOU MORE AND SEEING HOW YOU PROVE THAT I CAN TRUST YOU ALWAYS.

AMEN

Trust in the LORD with all your heart and lean not on your own understanding.

PROVERBS 3:5

But blessed is the one who trusts in the LORD, whose confidence is in him.

JEREMIAH 17:7

Look at my hands and my feet. It is I myself! Touch me and see; a ghost does not have flesh and bones, as you see I have.

LUKE 24:39

Offer the sacrifices of the righteous and trust in the LORD.

PSALMS 4:5

Some trust in chariots and some in horses, but we trust in the name of the Lord our God.

PSALMS 20:7

WORLDLINESS

We live in a world where possessions seem to dominate what we value. We see the houses, the cars, and the vacations of other men. Often that leads to envy or a desire to get to where others are. The reality is, what we possess is not as important as who we are. As godly men, we are called to not be friends with the world, meaning we shouldn't value worldly possessions over our relationship with God and people. I don't think God has a problem with us having possessions as much as he has a problem with possessions having us. This is the worldliness we should seek to resist.

Prayer

LORD,

WHAT A GIFT IT IS TO HAVE POSSESSIONS THAT CAN MAKE OUR LIVES SIMPLER, EASIER, OR MORE CONVENIENT. I PRAY THAT I DON'T PRIORITIZE POSSESSIONS OVER PEOPLE OR THE WORLD OVER THE SPIRIT. I KNOW THE LURE THAT WORLDLINESS BRINGS. I SEEK YOU TODAY AND ASK FOR YOUR SPIRIT TO GUIDE ME TO BE A GOOD STEWARD OF WHAT YOU'VE GIVEN ME.

AMEN

Set your minds on things that are above, not on things that are on earth.

COLOSSIANS 3:2

Do not love the world or the things in the world. If anyone loves the world, the love of the Father is not in him.

1 JOHN 2:15

Do not store up for yourselves treasures on earth, where moths and vermin destroy, and where thieves break in and steal.

MATTHEW 6:19

Why should fools have money in hand to buy wisdom, when they are not able to understand it?

PROVERBS 17:16

Those who want to get rich fall into temptation and a trap and into many foolish and harmful desires that plunge people into ruin and destruction. For the love of money is a root of all kinds of evil. Some people, eager for money, have wandered from the faith and pierced themselves with many griefs.

1 TIMOTHY 6:9-11

A Final Prayer for Guidance

HEAVENLY FATHER,

I ASK FOR YOUR CLEAR AND LOVING GUIDANCE IN EVERY STEP I TAKE. HELP ME TO TRUST YOU EVEN WHEN THE PATH IS UNCERTAIN, KNOWING YOU SEE BEYOND WHAT I CAN. LEAD ME BY YOUR SPIRIT AND ALIGN MY HEART WITH YOUR WILL.

AMEN